SOVEREIGNS

Sitting Bull and the Resistance of the Free Lakotas

ROBERT M. UTLEY

UNIVERSITY OF NEBRASKA PRESS | LINCOLN

Manufactured in the United States of America ∞

Publication of this volume was assisted by a grant from the Friends of the University of Nebraska Press.

Library of Congress Cataloging-in-Publication Data
Names: Utley, Robert M., 1929– author.
Title: The last sovereigns: Sitting Bull and the resistance of the free Lakotas / Robert M. Utley.
Description: Lincoln: University of Nebraska Press, [2020] | Includes bibliographical references and index.
Identifiers: LCCN 2019053439
ISBN 9781496220226 (hardback)
ISBN 9781496222787 (epub)
ISBN 9781496222794 (mobi)
ISBN 9781496222800 (pdf)
Subjects: LCSH: Sitting Bull, 1831–1890. | Lakota Indians—Canada—Biography. | Lakota Indians—Canada—Social conditions—19th century. | Indians of North America—Government relations—1869–1934. | LCGFT: Biographies.
Classification: LCC E99.T34 U85 2020 | DDC 978.004/97520092 [B]—dc23
LC record available at https://lccn.loc.gov/2019053439

Set in Vesper by Mikala R. Kolander.

Contents

Illustrations

Preface

The Sioux chief Sitting Bull is arguably the greatest Indian chief of all the tribes that roamed the American West in the nineteenth century. In the decades since his death, his name has become known to most Americans and treasured by many as the supreme embodiment of Sioux values. He lived from 1831 to 1890.

Sitting Bull's final four years as a leader and a free man were spent in Canada. He was forty-six years old when he led one thousand of his Hunkpapa Sioux people across the "medicine line" and sought refuge in Canada. The time was May 1877, nearly a year after the Battle of the Little Bighorn, in which Sioux and Cheyenne warriors overwhelmed the Seventh Cavalry and killed "Long Hair" Custer and more than two hundred of his men.

People wrongly blamed Sitting Bull for that catastrophe. But his name had been well-known to the American people for nearly a decade. He had committed depredations against white settlers and fought the U.S. Army. So notorious was he as the leading "hostile" of the Northern Plains that he was now *the* man to get. The army tried hard, but Sitting Bull and his following made it to Canada, where they believed they would be safe.

Here these Sioux, also known as Lakotas, met a different breed of white man. Instead of blue coats, they wore scarlet coats. Instead of responding with force, they greeted the newcomers warmly. Organized only four years earlier, the North-West Mounted Police came west with the mission of overseeing Canada's native Indians and maintaining law and order in the newly opened Northwest Territories.

The first redcoat to meet Sitting Bull was Maj. James Morrow Walsh. Not only did he gain Sitting Bull's confidence, but Sitting Bull gained Walsh's confidence. Their relationship grew into one of friendship.

The refugees had been granted permission to remain in Canada on condition that they obey the Queen's laws and never cross the boundary into the United States, then return to Canada. Although that gradually became honored in the breach, the Mounties had extended too warm a welcome. Canadian policy was to persuade the refugees to return to the United States. Persuading Sitting Bull became Walsh's primary mission.

Sitting Bull treasured his freedom and his adherence to the old way of life. If he went back, he feared that the Americans would punish him for killing Custer and his soldiers. He was a wanted man, and he knew that they would confine him to a reservation where he would lose his freedom.

The drama of his resistance was existential and very real. His people were hungry and in time would face starvation. The buffalo herds on which they depended for sustenance were dwindling. To add to this threat, the indigenous Canadian tribes also depended on the scarce buffalo, and they regarded the Lakotas as interlopers preying on their food source. Hostility dogged Sitting Bull from these tribes throughout the Canadian years.

Although simply stated, all of the elements of Sitting Bull's Canadian life involved complex decision-making that troubled him constantly. He was the great Lakota chief responsible for thousands of resistors under grave threat constantly. A tale of drama, tragedy, success, failure, poignancy, friendship, hostility, controversy, dispute, and a host of highs and lows defined the story of the last free Lakotas and their effort to create a new life in a new home.

This book began several years ago as a simple "story of a friendship" between Sitting Bull and Major Walsh. As I worked on it, however, a larger story took shape. The friendship still played its part, but it was overshadowed by Sitting Bull's struggle to remain free, to resist coercion into the white man's ways, and to continue to live in safety the way Lakotas had always lived. This story of resistance and struggle became the dominant story. The story of the last free Lakotas gives us a new appreciation of Native resistance in the waning years of Indigenous free life. The drama of these four years is at times heroic and thrilling, at other times heartbreaking and brutal. As the fortunes of these last free Lakotas change, we follow Sitting Bull to the climax of both his life and the free life of the Lakotas.

The Last Sovereigns is an outgrowth of a full biography of Sitting Bull that I wrote in the late 1980s: *The Lance and the Shield: The Life and Times of Sitting Bull*. The Canadian years are treated in that book too, but not in the detail I have always believed they deserved. Sitting Bull's character and personality emerge more clearly during the Canadian resistance. Several other books have chronicled these four years, but in my judgment only one has merit. It is included in the bibliography under the name Manzione.

My biography was reissued in 2008 as a paperback, with the title *Sitting Bull: The Life and Times of an American Patriot*. "American Patriot" applies to Sitting Bull only in the ironic sense that, unlike some American Indian chiefs, his certitude in the validity of the traditional Sioux way of life—in other words, the first *American* way of life—never dimmed.

Acknowledgments

Since many of those who helped me were the archivists and librarians of the depositories I visited in preparation for the full biography of Sitting Bull, I cannot now thank them properly. Even so, I extend my thanks once again. One who helped me then is still active and deserves high praise for sharing his papers, artwork, and knowledge of the North-West Mounted Police. He is the reigning expert on the police, and he is still in a sharing mode: George Kush of Monarch, Alberta.

But the person who deserves my most serious appreciation is Christopher Rogers. Our relationship started years ago when he was an editor at Yale University Press, and he guided me through several books published by the press. He is now my literary agent and has taken great interest in this book. My editors at the University of Nebraska Press, Matthew Bokovoy, Heather Stauffer, Ann Baker, and Matt Goodwin, have expertly seen this manuscript become a book. Many thanks to all. Bill Nelson deserves high credit for the excellent maps.

THE LAST SOVEREIGNS

1

Sitting Bull

Rosebud River, Montana, 1869. Chiefs of all seven Lakota tribes gathered at the call of the powerful Hunkpapa chief Four Horns. The seven tribes—Hunkpapa, Oglala, Miniconjou, Sans Arc, Two Kettle, Brule, and Blackfeet—maintained loose bonds of friendship with one another and, when necessary, alliances in warfare against other tribes. But each followed its own hierarchy of chiefs. Four Horns worried that the previous year's treaty with the Wasichus, the white people, would disturb the solidarity of the Lakota tribes. He proposed that they choose a head chief of all the tribes, one concerned with all decisions of war and peace. Such a post had never existed, but if any of the chiefs harbored doubts they did not voice them.

Four Horns nominated his nephew Sitting Bull, head chief of the Hunkpapas, thirty-nine years old.

Four Horns conducted an election. Each chief voted for Sitting Bull. Four Horns then addressed the new chief: "For your bravery on the battlefields and as the greatest warrior of our bands, we have elected you as our war chief, leader of the entire Lakota nation. When you tell us to fight, we shall fight, when you tell us to make peace, we shall make peace."

Sitting Bull, singing songs of his own composition, led a grand parade through the village. He had achieved the highest distinction of his life.[1]

An even higher distinction, however, lay beyond his own Lakota world. History has judged him to be among the greatest chiefs of western American Indians—perhaps the greatest chief of all. Chief Joseph of the Nez Perce was a great chief, as were Cochise and Mangas Coloradas of the Apaches; Dull Knife, Two Moons, and Roman Nose of the Cheyennes; Quanah Parker and Buffalo Hump of the Comanches; and Lone Wolf and Satanta of the Kiowas. When Sitting Bull lost his freedom, the last of the Sioux to surrender autonomy, he was the last of the Indians of the West except for a handful of Apaches who followed Geronimo, who surrendered five years later.

Singular as Sitting Bull's story is, he was not alone among the chiefs named in struggling to break the grip of the white man over his life and destiny. They all shared that struggle in one way or another. All longed to sustain the sovereignty and way of life that they or their ancestors had enjoyed before the white man arrived, and all succeeded either briefly or for a longer period until they met the same fate as Sitting Bull. An expanding group of distinguished scholars probe the quest of most of the tribes that now inhabit North America for cultural, political, and geographical autonomy. As this story recounts, Sitting Bull was the last.

Tatanka-Iyotanka, his Lakota name, represented an unyielding buffalo bull sitting on his haunches. Sitting Bull's life reflected the image: unyielding against the forces that would harm his people.

Born in 1831, by the 1860s Sitting Bull had ascended to head chief of the Hunkpapa tribe of the Teton Sioux, or Lakotas. An exceptional leader, he bore a host of war honors and exerted potent influence in tribal councils and men's societies. Nobility, patriotism, and devotion to his people heightened his stature, and the spirituality of the Holy Man broadened it. Early in his adult life he evolved into the embodiment of the four cardinal virtues that defined Lakota manhood: bravery, fortitude, generosity, and wisdom. By age forty-five, not yet head chief of all the tribes, Sitting Bull had become an "Old Man Chief," one so distinguished and valuable that his people expected him to stay out of battle.

Power and prestige never diluted Sitting Bull's human touch. Whether speaking to a tribe or individual, an adult or child, he always had time to advise, encourage, sympathize, explain, or simply converse. He loved his people and they loved him. In short, Sitting Bull was a paragon of Lakota leadership and humanity.[2]

Sitting Bull had reached this height of veneration largely through war, the principal means of developing and exhibiting the cardinal virtue of bravery. The traditional Hunkpapa enemies were the Crow and Assiniboine tribes. These tribes ranged west and north of the Hunkpapa domain along the Upper Missouri River.

During his early years Sitting Bull bore the name Slow. At age fourteen, however, he attached himself to a party of ten men setting forth on a foray into Crow country. War parties often allowed novices to go with them to tend to camp chores. When the warriors spotted a dozen Crows and charged, Slow joined them. He targeted one Crow who tried to break away from his companions. Overtaking his quarry, Slow smashed him on the head with his tomahawk and knocked him from his pony. Although another Hunkpapa dismounted and killed the Crow, Slow had counted first coup. A first coup, especially by one so young, was a singular triumph. It catapulted him to the rank of warrior. He could now wear a white eagle feather in his hair. In celebration his father conferred his own name on his son: Tatanka-Iyotanka, Sitting Bull. Counting first coup on an enemy was Sitting Bull's first war honor, the first of many that would stamp him as the epitome of the first of the cardinal virtues: bravery.[3]

Sitting Bull's war record unfolded swiftly. Only a year later, at age fifteen, he fought in a battle with Flathead warriors. With both sides arrayed in lines facing each other, the fifteen-year-old ran the "daring line," a common means of demonstrating bravery by galloping the length of the enemy line and exposing himself to their fire. Bullets and arrows sought the youth as he spurred his horse in front of the Flathead warriors. One hit him in the foot. The wound qualified him for a second feather, this one red.[4]

Sitting Bull became so adept at fighting that enemy tribesmen recognized him. On his swift horse Bloated Jaw, he usually got into the battle first. Crow, Assiniboine, and Flathead warriors noticed whom they faced and put up a confused fight or fled altogether. Exploiting the value of his name, his followers shouted a battle cry: *Tatanka-Iyotanka tahoksila*—"We are Sitting Bull's boys!"[5]

In 1857 Sitting Bull's war record elevated him to the rank of war chief of the Hunkpapa tribe. In the same year, at a tribal gathering at the mouth of Grand River, four distinguished men placed his name in nomination for head chief of the Hunkpapa tribe. The tribe approved. An elaborate ceremony validated the choice. At age twenty-six Sitting Bull was both head chief and war chief of his tribe.[6]

Sitting Bull sat in the tribal councils not only as war chief and head chief of the Hunkpapas, and later of all the tribes, but also, adding to his stature and influence, as a Wichasha Wakan, a Holy Man. Visions, dreams, and instructions from learned advisors prepared him for this distinction, but the test of the Sun Dance loomed above all others. Sitting Bull danced his first in his mid-twenties. With skewers pierced both in chest and back, he danced around a pole, straining to break free, staring at the sun, and beseeching Wakantanka, the Great Mystery, to favor his people. Before the skewers tore through his chest and back, he received an answer: "Wakantanka gives you what you ask for / Wakantanka will grant your wish." One Bull recalled that after this first Sun Dance, "Sitting Bull danced often. He wanted to learn to love his god and his people." He danced so frequently that in later years heavy scars marked his chest, back, and arms.[7]

As one of many examples of the Wichasha Wakan calling, Sitting Bull was a prominent dreamer, singer, and composer. Most of his dreams, and the songs he created to express them, centered on buffalo, wolves, and birds. He had a special affinity for birds, expressed in one incident. As he lay sleeping at the foot of a tree, he dreamed that a colorful bird perched above him. Interrupting the crashing noise of an approaching beast, the bird instructed the sleeping man not to move. A large bear strode past without noticing Sitting Bull. When he awoke, he saw a woodpecker pecking at the tree trunk and watching him. On the spot he composed a song. Spreading his arms toward the bird, he sang: "Pretty bird you have seen me and took pity on me / Amongst the tribes to live, you wish for me / Ye bird tribes from henceforth, always my relation shall be."[8]

While fighting Crows and Assiniboines, the Hunkpapas dealt with another people: Wasichus, white people. They appeared on the Upper Missouri even before Sitting Bull's birth, but these whites posed no threat. On the contrary, they tended trading posts that Sitting Bull and his tribesmen visited often to exchange buffalo robes for the white man's manufactures. These items made life more convenient than reliance on their own fabricated utensils. They could also acquire rifles and ammunition, which made hunting easier than the bow and arrow and were essential in fighting the Crows and Assiniboines. Even while engaging in this trade, however, Sitting Bull fretted over the growing dependence of his people on the white man's tools.

The principal trading post was Fort Pierre on the Missouri River. Those who operated this and other trading posts were not the kind of whites who began to appear in the 1850s. Many were French-Canadians who got along well with the Indians. Those who arrived in the 1850s, however, did endanger the Lakota way of life. They were officials of the white man's government.

At first these new whites only wanted the tribes to stop fighting one another because it imperiled the white people who were moving west. In 1851 the officials called on all the northern plains tribes to gather at Fort Laramie, on the Platte River, and make a treaty. Many tribes responded, mainly because the white officials handed out food and other gifts. The officials explained that the Indians would promise in the treaty to quit fighting and remain within boundaries drawn on paper. In return they would be rewarded each year with issues of provisions. The chiefs readily made their marks on the paper, although they had almost no understanding of what the marks meant and paid no attention to the promises the marks represented.

Neither Sitting Bull nor any other Hunkpapa traveled down to Fort Laramie to sign the treaty. Even so, government agents came up the river each year to deposit the rations promised in the treaty. They also scolded the Indians for violating the treaty. This strange behavior opened schisms in all the Lakota tribes: should they continue to fight their enemies or make peace and take the white man's gifts? Sitting Bull, steadily acquiring more war honors and larger stature and influence, had no intention of calling off raiding hostile tribes or whites or any other people caught at a disadvantage.

In 1855 the Lakotas confronted still another kind of white men: the government's blue-coated soldiers—*Long Knives*. To the south, near Fort Laramie, a brash young officer blundered into a fight with the Brule chief Conquering Bear and lost his entire command of thirty men, himself included. Conquering Bear was killed in the fight. In revenge, an army marched up the Platte River, slaughtered many people, then marched through Lakota country to the Missouri River at Fort Pierre. Other soldiers came up the river on steamboats and disembarked at Fort Pierre. The soldier chief was demanding, ruthless, and tyrannical. The Lakotas called him "Mad Bear."[9]

Mad Bear (Gen. William S. Harney) imposed harsh rule on the Lakotas. Under the guise of a treaty, he defined severe rules by which they were to live and appointed a "head chief" of each tribe to ensure that they obeyed the rules. Turmoil roiled all the Lakota tribes, but Sitting Bull took little or no part in the controversies. He continued to accumulate war honors, although not against the soldiers of the feared Mad Bear.

Although Mad Bear soon moved elsewhere, he left behind in Sitting Bull an intense hatred of white people. It worsened in the 1860s when gold was discovered in western Montana. Gold-seekers ascended the Missouri River in steamboats and trekked westward by land. At the same time, Santee Sioux in Minnesota revolted against their white overlords and carried the war with white soldiers westward toward the Hunkpapas. The Hunkpapas fought in some of these hostilities, both east of the Missouri River and west as far as the Bighorn Mountains.

The white people wanted peace, but on their own terms. These nomadic people should give up their freedom, settle down and become farmers, on reservations carved out of their own lands. The "Great Father" would send agents to issue rations, teach them how to farm, and instruct them in the habits of "civilization."

In 1868, at Fort Laramie, government officials concluded such a treaty with the Oglala chief Red Cloud. The treaty defined a Great Sioux Reservation consisting of all the present state of South Dakota west of the Missouri River. West of the reservation, in a hazy legal stratagem, the treaty identified an "unceded Indian territory" extending to the crest of the Bighorn Mountains. Here those who disliked drawing rations at the government "gift houses" could follow the buffalo as long as they existed.

Sitting Bull did not sign this treaty or any other. He had come quickly to detest the "white eyes" and their reservations. Their "gift houses" held no appeal for one who had been reared on the meat of the buffalo and whose way of life had been largely shaped by the buffalo. "Look at me," he declared to a group of Assiniboines. "See if I am poor, or my people either. The whites may get me at last, as you say, but I will have good times until then. You are fools to make yourselves slaves to a piece of fat bacon, some hard-tack, and a little sugar and coffee."[10]

Many of them did enslave themselves. In the years after 1868 the seven Lakota tribes gravitated into two groups: those who settled on the reservation and those who remained in the unceded territory. The latter, called "winter roamers," or simply "hunters," followed the old life, Sitting Bull conspicuous among them. Many of those who lived on the reservation moved west in the spring to join their kinsmen for a summer of the old life; and in the winter some of the hunting bands rode to the agencies to visit their kin and eat some of the agent's beef.

This was precisely the disruption of Lakota solidarity that Four Horns had foreseen and that led to Sitting Bull's elevation to head chief of all the Lakotas in 1869. Over the next few years, as the threat of the Wasichus grew more acute, the winter roamers, now including the Northern Cheyennes, coalesced under Sitting Bull's leadership. They also recognized Crazy Horse of the Oglalas as the leading war chief. The Cheyenne Wooden Leg explained how the new scheme functioned:

Councils of chiefs of all the tribal circles were held sometimes at one camp circle and sometimes at another. In each case, heralds announced the meeting and told where it would be held. Each tribe operated its own internal government, the same as if it were entirely separated from the others. The chiefs of the different tribes met together as equals. There was only one who was considered as being above the others. This was Sitting Bull. He was recognized as the one old man chief of all the camps combined.[11]

The winter roamers wanted nothing more than to be left alone in the buffalo ranges and occasionally to visit the trading posts along the Missouri River. Sitting Bull and Crazy Horse regarded as their homeland the mountains and plains that the white officials called the unceded territory. The two agreed that they would fight only in defense. They would quit attacking the army forts on the Missouri River, but they would fight for their homeland if invaded.

An invasion seemed imminent in the summer of 1871. They knew about the iron horse because they sometimes raided the ones chuffing up the Platte River Valley in Nebraska. More ominously, they saw another railway advancing across the prairies east of the Missouri River. Surveying parties for this railway, the Northern Pacific, appeared on the Elk River—the Yellowstone. Long Knives guarded them. Angry Lakotas watched and in the autumn served notice at a Missouri River fort that any further encroachment would be resisted.

In summer 1872 the bluecoats came back. The Lakotas resisted. They attacked one group and so frightened them that they abandoned their mission. This was the Battle of Arrow Creek, August 14, 1872, where Sitting Bull's bravest and most memorable feat occurred. The warriors attacked soldiers fortified in a dry river bed. As the two sides exchanged fire, Sitting Bull calmly collected his pipe regalia and slowly walked out between the lines. He sat and began to fill his pipe. "Who other Indians wish to smoke with me come," he shouted. Four warriors, including his nephew White Bull, hesitantly ventured forth and sat with him. Bullets laced the air and kicked dust around them as they lit their pipes and smoked. When all the tobacco had

burned, Sitting Bull thoroughly cleaned out the pipe bowl and saun-
tered back to his lines. The others ran back.[12]

While Sitting Bull and his warriors engaged the soldiers at Arrow
Creek, farther east the efficient Hunkpapa war chief Gall was engaging the soldiers who had guarded the eastern party of railroad sur-
veyors. Shortly Sitting Bull arrived, and he joined Gall in setting up
an early morning ambush while the soldiers were breaking camp
for the day's march. Several hundred warriors charged on horseback
while two hundred more fired down from positions on the adjacent
bluffs. The soldiers corralled their wagon train and formed in line.
Others tried to climb the bluffs to dislodge the warriors firing there.
As the fight raged Sitting Bull ascended the bluffs, stood behind a
large rock, and shouted his name. If a railroad were built, he declared,
"there would be no more Indians." Therefore he had summoned all
the tribes, who would soon come and kill all the soldiers and railroad workers.[13]

The soldiers came again the following summer. Sitting Bull's village
of about four hundred lodges of Hunkpapas and Miniconjous stood
on the north bank of the Yellowstone, in the path of the advancing
soldiers. This year they were horsemen under the officer they would
soon know as "Long Hair"—George Armstrong Custer. A party of
warriors sought to decoy the advance guard into an ambush. Long
Hair himself commanded these cavalrymen. He pretended to be
decoyed, but at the last moment swiftly took cover in a copse of
trees and repulsed repeated attacks until the main column arrived
and fired a cannon.

The Lakota village moved swiftly up the valley and crossed to the
south side near the mouth of the Bighorn River. Sitting Bull sent
runners to summon more warriors from a large village on the lower
Bighorn. With Oglalas, Sans Arcs, and Cheyennes added to his force,
Sitting Bull returned to resume the fight. Early on August 10 he strung
a line of warriors on the rocky slopes across the river from the cavalry
camp and opened fire. The soldiers returned fire, and the two sides
fired at each other most of the day. Sitting Bull and White Bull sat
on the incline watching the firing. Twice a contingent of warriors

crossed the river to entice the soldiers into a fight. Both times they were successful but were driven from the field by the cavalry. Late in the day infantry arrived with artillery, which blasted the slope opposite the soldier bivouac with cannon shell. The battle ended, with all the Indians drawing off to the southwest.[14]

The clashes of 1873 forced Sitting Bull's followers out of the Yellowstone Valley. Even so, the railroad people quit coming. Sitting Bull and the chiefs believed that they had won. They had not. Forces beyond their comprehension achieved that. The Panic of 1873 had plunged the Northern Pacific into bankruptcy and halted construction.

But the white people had not lost interest in Indian land. In summer 1874 soldiers under Long Hair Custer marched from a new fort on the Missouri River, named Fort Abraham Lincoln, and entered the Black Hills, a special place to the Lakotas that lay within the Great Sioux Reservation. This expedition met no resistance, but it did confirm what white people suspected: the Black Hills contained gold. The soldiers had scarcely left before gold-seekers swarmed into the hills.

Four Horns's apprehensions proved correct. Tensions on the reservation pitted chiefs and headmen against government agents. Although the Northern Pacific Railway had been stopped by financial breakdown, both Gen. William T. Sherman, head of the army, and Gen. Philip H. Sheridan, commanding the Military Division of the Missouri in Chicago, knew that they would have to fight for the railroad. Bankruptcy postponed the conflict, but the Black Hills hastened it.

Soldiers in the Black Hills did not violate the Treaty of 1868, and General Sheridan wanted to build a military post there to keep watch on the Red Cloud and Spotted Tail agencies to the south. The Indians resented the invasion but did not contest it. Prospectors in the hills did antagonize them; they called Custer's route "The Thieves' Road." When the government tried to buy the hills from them in 1875, Sitting Bull joined with the other hunting chiefs to reject the offer. Pres. Ulysses S. Grant faced a dilemma: honor treaty requirements or find a way to open the hills to miners.

That set the stage for the Great Sioux War that began in 1876. To solve the president's quandary, top generals and officials of the Indian office contrived a cause for war: Sitting Bull's warriors were intimidating the friendly tribes along the Upper Missouri River. Runners set forth from the agencies with an ultimatum ordering the Lakota tribes to report to their agencies by February 1, 1876, or the soldiers would march to force them in. None of the people contacted took the order seriously. Moving their villages in winter was difficult and hazardous, and they could talk to government agents when convenient. The deadline came and went, and the soldiers marched.

Reacting to the threat of the soldiers, the tribes of winter roamers came together. During spring 1876 about five hundred lodges moved among the rivers flowing north in the Powder River country, seeking buffalo. They looked to Sitting Bull for leadership, as recalled by the Cheyenne Wooden Leg:

He had come into admiration by all Indians as a man whose medicine was good—that is, as a man having a kind heart and good judgment as to the best course of conduct. He was considered as being altogether brave, but peaceable. He was strong in religion—Indian religion. He made medicine many times. He prayed and fasted and whipped his flesh into submission to the will of the Great Medicine.[15]

Sitting Bull did indeed whip his flesh in appeal to Wakantanka. Ascending Rosebud River in late May 1876, he slipped into his role as Holy Man. Two prayer sessions yielded visions of soldiers approaching. In the visions he implored Wakantanka for help and promised his own flesh in return. To make good his pledge, in early June he laid out a Sun Dance circle farther up the river, near where he had been made head chief of all the tribes seven years earlier. In an elaborate ritual, he seated himself with his back to the Sun Dance pole and stretched his arms and legs flat against the earth. His adopted Assiniboine brother, Jumping Bull, performed the task. Working his way up the arms with an awl, he gouged fifty pieces of flesh from each. Afterward, blood streaming from his arms, Sitting Bull rose. Gazing intently at the sun, he danced around the pole until he fainted. When he awoke he described a vision: many soldiers charging the village but with their heads down and feet pointed up to the sky. "These soldiers do not possess ears," he declared, "They are to die."[16]

Sunday, June 25, 1876, was a clear, hot, sunny day in the valley of Montana's Greasy Grass River, which the white man's maps labeled the Little Bighorn. Six tribal circles of Lakotas and one of Northern Cheyennes, the coalition of winter roamers, sprawled for nearly three miles down the narrow valley, rimmed on the east by the snow-fed river. The Hunkpapas occupied the extreme upper end of the village, the Cheyennes the lower. In between rose the lodges of Blackfeet, Miniconjou, Sans Arc, Oglala, and Brule. It was an unusually large village: seven thousand people, two thousand warriors, housed in thousands of tipis and wickyups. In the past few days, Indians arriving from the agencies had swollen the village.

Sitting Bull's lodge, on the southern edge of the Hunkpapa circle, sheltered twelve people besides the chief: two wives, his mother, two teenage daughters, three sons, two stepsons, his sister, and the brother of his two wives. He treasured his family.[17]

On this hot summer day, some of the men rode up to the benchland west of the valley to tend their grazing pony herds. After a night of dancing and feasting, others dozed in their tipis or beneath the tall cottonwood trees shading the river bank. Children played in the cool waters of the stream. Women dug for wild roots.

In the middle of the afternoon a current of anxiety ran through the village, disturbing the peaceful scene. Shortly heralds rode through each circle. "They are charging, the chargers are coming!" they cried.[18] They were coming, and they were soon within sight of Sitting Bull's lodge. "I heard a terrific volley of carbines," recalled Moving Robe Woman. "The bullets shattered the tipi poles. Women and children were running away from the gunfire. In the tumult I heard old men and women singing death songs for their warriors who were now ready to attack the soldiers."[19] One Bull and White Bull galloped

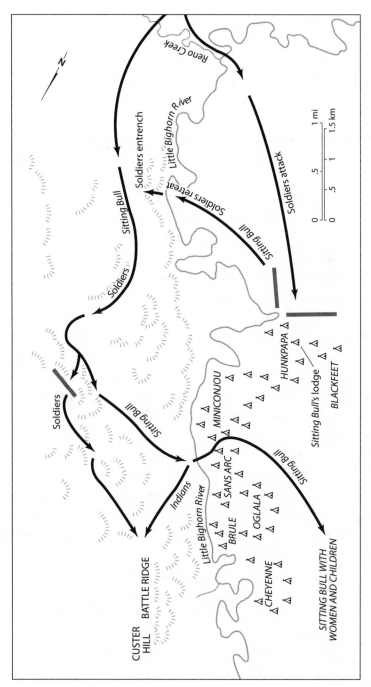

Map 1. Sitting Bull at Little Bighorn, June 25, 1876. Bill Nelson Cartography.

down from the bench to help their uncle prepare for battle. Old man chiefs were not supposed to fight, but he had to defend himself and family. Astride a large black horse, brandishing a Winchester rifle, he hurried among warriors pouring from their tipis. "Brave up, boys, it will be a hard time. Brave up!" he shouted.[20]

But the "chargers" quit charging. They got off their horses and lay on the ground firing at the Hunkpapa tipis. Sitting Bull dismounted and joined others, including the venerated chief Four Horns, in a shallow draw from which to shoot back. White Bull called this "standstill shooting."

Soon warriors from the other tribal circles began reaching the scene, many following the indomitable Oglala Crazy Horse. The standstill shooting ended.

Crazy Horse and the arriving warriors drove the soldiers into timber enclosed by a bend in the river. Now on the defensive, the troopers fought back, though ineffectively. In about twenty minutes they mounted and burst from the timber, racing across the open valley toward a line of high bluffs on the other side of the river, every man for himself. Warriors rode among them, striking them down as they sought to save themselves. They jumped into and crossed the river, then climbed the bluffs to the top. They had lost thirty killed and thirteen wounded.

Sitting Bull had not ridden in this rout of the soldiers. As long as they remained in the valley, he fired his Winchester at them and encouraged his young men to fight. After the soldiers had reached the top of the bluffs, he rode about the valley examining the carnage, then crossed the river and climbed one of the ravines scouring the bluffs. At the top, soldiers had formed into a defensive circle and were exchanging fire with Indians scaling the heights. One Bull recalled that his uncle "was back on the hill sort of directing things, though he himself did not go into the fight at all"—appropriate behavior for an old man chief. He even remarked to One Bull that the warriors should let the soldiers go back home and tell the whites what had occurred on these bluffs.[21]

But there were still more soldiers to fight. They had been glimpsed downstream, opposite the lower end of the village. "The word passed among the Indians like a whirlwind," said Red Horse, "and they all started to attack this new party, leaving the troops on the hill."[22]

Accompanied by One Bull, Sitting Bull joined the other warriors hastening north along the ridgetops. Soon they spotted the new threat: many soldiers already fighting against converging warriors. Instead of joining the fight, Sitting Bull left One Bull and worked his way down a broad coulee to the river, splashed across, and rode to where the women and children had gathered beyond the Cheyenne circle. He saw his duty as helping to protect the women and children rather than exposing himself in the battle that he could see developing on a high ridge across the river.[23]

Smoke and dust obscured the details of the fighting rolling along the crest of the ridge. Within an hour Sitting Bull learned the outcome. The warriors had annihilated the entire contingent of soldiers, including "Long Hair" Custer. Sitting Bull's prayers had been answered and his prophecy validated by the greatest triumph in the history of his people.

The soldiers who had first attacked the village remained on the bluffs four miles to the south. Warriors rode in that direction to resume the battle. They found that more soldiers had arrived to strengthen the ones who had retreated from the valley. They had scooped out shallow rifle pits, and fired at the returning warriors. Sitting Bull and One Bull took station on a high ridge overlooking the defenders and fired shots at them. Shortly, however, Sitting Bull went back to his lodge in the valley. Here he witnessed the sad spectacle of dead and wounded warriors, draped over the backs of horses, borne down from the heights. The battle that had killed so many soldiers had also brought grief to families in the valley.

The fight for the hilltop resumed early the next morning. Sitting Bull remained in his lodge until noon, when he climbed the bluffs. Again, he believed the fighting should end: "Let them go now so some can go home and spread the news. I just saw more soldiers coming."[24]

More soldiers were coming, south up the valley. People in the village discovered their approach and at once began to dismantle their tipis and pack for a hasty flight. Sitting Bull returned to his lodge and with his family joined the procession up the valley, away from the oncoming soldiers.

The battle was over, but the war wasn't. The white people were furious. They could hardly believe that Long Hair Custer and 225 men of the Seventh Cavalry regiment had met with such a catastrophe. Even the generals were at first skeptical. When the truth dawned on the nation, Sitting Bull personified the calamity. Fresh soldiers poured up the Yellowstone to join with those already in the field. Revenge was the watchword. As they pursued the conquest of the Lakotas, one name loomed above all other chiefs: Sitting Bull. He was the man to get.

He was not easy to get. The great Lakota coalition split into several components, some bearing south, others north. Sitting Bull chose the latter.

Word that buffalo ranged the plains north of the Yellowstone lured Sitting Bull north and across the Yellowstone, which he forded on October 10, 1876. Miniconjous and Sans Arcs accompanied the Hunkpapas. The next day they spotted a large encampment of army supply wagons opposite the mouth of Glendive Creek. Warriors attacked but were driven off by the soldiers. Afterward the wagons formed into a train and began moving up the river. On October 15 and 16 One Bull and fellow warriors swarmed around them, only to be thwarted again by "walk-a-heap" soldiers—infantry armed with long high-powered rifles.

In the Lakota village the chiefs debated whether to try to make peace with the soldier chief. Sitting Bull still harbored the same thoughts he had on the Little Bighorn bluffs, when he advised his men to let the soldiers go. He had not joined in the attack on the soldier encampment, nor in the subsequent assaults of his warriors. Now he favored a gesture toward the soldiers.

In the camp was a mixed-blood man named John Bruguier. He had ridden into the Lakota camp a month earlier seeking sanctuary from the law. Sitting Bull allowed him to remain. Because he wore flapping leg chaps, the Indians called him "Big Leggings." Sitting Bull dictated a message, which Bruguier wrote down. It was tacked to a stake and driven into the center of the road the wagon train was following.

> I want to know what you are doing on this road. You scare all the buffalo away. I want to hunt on this place. I want you to turn back from here. If you don't I will fight you again. I want you to leave what you have got here, and turn back from here.

> I am your friend, Sitting Bull

> I mean all the rations you have got and some powder. Wish you would write as soon as you can.

They were Big Leggings's awkward words but Sitting Bull's thoughts, highly presumptuous but not without modest result. Two emissaries advanced on the halted train. The soldier chief would not talk with them, only Sitting Bull. Reluctantly, Sitting Bull joined with several other chiefs and walked to the train. He gestured to his companions to do the talking. They pressed the officer for food and ammunition—and peace. He replied that they had fired a lot of their ammunition today attacking his train; and moreover, he had no authority to make peace. Nor would he feed them, although when the train continued up the Yellowstone he left behind token supplies of hard bread and bacon.[25]

Gathering the paltry supplies piled next to the road, the Lakotas moved farther to the northwest and on October 20 discovered a herd of buffalo. They encamped on the heights dividing the Missouri and Yellowstone Rivers and sallied forth to attack the herd. Almost at once, however, scouts brought word of still more soldiers advancing on their trail. The Lakotas gathered on the ridge and watched the soldiers form in line of battle. To ward off an attack, Sitting Bull hazarded another talk with the soldiers. Two emissaries rode toward them with a white flag. "These troops were on the warpath," said one of the two. "We ran great risk in going to them, but we went directly to them."[26]

After an hour of confusion on both sides, a parley was arranged. Groups from each side advanced toward each other. Accompanied by an array of chiefs, Sitting Bull led his party. They bore no arms, although a mounted contingent of armed warriors followed. The day was sunny and clear but bitter cold. A heavy buffalo robe covered Sitting Bull's plainly attired frame. The soldier chief and his staff rode toward them. They dismounted and hesitantly sat on buffalo robes spread on the ground. Big Leggings stood nearby to interpret.

Sitting Bull faced an officer who was to play a large role in his life. To ward off the cold, he wore a fur cap and a long overcoat trimmed in bear fur. "Bear Coat," the Indians dubbed him, a name that endured through four years of contention and battle.

He was Col. Nelson A. Miles, whose Fifth Infantry regiment was building winter quarters on the Yellowstone at the mouth of Tongue River. Tall and well-proportioned, with a neat black mustache, he was intensely ambitious, determined to gather all the power and rank he could. His wife's uncle, Gen. William T. Sherman, headed the army. Bear Coat intended to stay on the northern plains throughout the winter and carry the war to Sitting Bull—to capture or kill him. Sitting Bull would find this man a dangerous opponent, the more so because he was inclined to stretch his orders to the limit and beyond to swell his reputation.

The talks lasted for two days. Amid the many words, two thoughts prevailed: Bear Coat demanded that Sitting Bull surrender and do as the government wished; Sitting Bull steadfastly refused and told Bear Coat to leave him alone. Frustrated, at the end of the second day both sides formed for battle. The soldiers attacked, and the Indians fought back from higher positions. The fighting continued inconclusively for two days as the Indians made their way forty-two miles back to the Yellowstone, abandoning food and camp equipage on the way. En route Sitting Bull and his immediate Hunkpapa following peeled off and turned back north; the Miniconjous and Sans Arcs crossed the river and surrendered to Miles.[27] Sitting Bull's nephew, White Bull, went with the Miniconjous because he had married into the Miniconjou tribe. One Bull remained with his uncle.

For Sitting Bull, the brutal winter of 1876–77 brought suffering from hunger, poverty, bitter cold with weeks of rain and snow, and repeated hasty moves to avoid Bear Coat's relentless campaign. The soldiers kept to the field all winter, ranging up and down the Missouri River where it flows east before turning south. On December 18 a unit of Miles's soldiers overtook Sitting Bull's village of about 120 lodges and attacked. The Indians abandoned their dwellings and fled south, the soldiers in pursuit. Left behind, besides ponies, food, and all other possessions, were piles of buffalo robes, which the soldiers took back to their winter quarters to have made into overcoats.[28]

Increasingly destitute, increasingly frightened by Bear Coat, Sitting Bull agonized in uncertainty. Increasingly he pondered taking refuge in Canada, the land of the White Mother. This option grew more appealing as Four Horns, Black Moon, and other Hunkpapa chiefs crossed the line late in 1876. In the Lakota mind the boundary took on almost spiritual meaning. "They told us that this line was considered holy," recounted one of the Lakotas. "They called that a holy trail. They believe things are different when you cross from one side to another. You are altogether different. On one side you are perfectly free to do as you please. On the other you are in danger."[29]

Sitting Bull did not view Canada in such simplistic terms. He did not want to leave his own country, and he avoided a decision even as his shrinking following moved closer to the holy line during the early months of 1877. On March 17 they crossed the Missouri River and pitched their shelters on the north bank. That night the winter's ice pack in the Missouri River broke up and sent a giant wall of water down the river. It swept over the Lakota camp and damaged or destroyed nearly all their possessions.

Everyone recognized that the time for decision was overdue. On April 10, sixty miles north of the Missouri, they convened a council of a dozen chiefs. Sitting Bull spoke in favor of continuing the war until the white soldiers surrendered. Not for the last time, his wishful thinking had converted fantasy into reality. Contradicting himself, he declared that he would cross the boundary and wait until he could discover how the people who had preceded him were treated.[30]

Sitting Bull had been in Canada before, principally to trade with the Red River mixed-bloods the Lakotas called Slotas. Now Canada posed uncertainties: were there enough buffalo to feed the Lakotas? Would the tribes native to Canada welcome or fight them? Would Canadian authorities treat them fairly? These and other unknowns plagued Sitting Bull and his followers, but all paled before the reality of poverty and constant fear of Bear Coat's soldiers suddenly dashing into their village—a village grown much smaller because so many of the Lakotas, including Four Horns and Black Moon, had already sought refuge in Canada.

Despite the conclusions reached in the chiefs' council of April 10, Sitting Bull and his people continued to move slowly northward. The village now counted 135 lodges, about a thousand people, and all suffered terribly from the Missouri River flood that tore through their dwellings. They edged up Milk River from its confluence with the Missouri, then turned north on Frenchmen's Creek. Early in May 1877 they crossed the *chanku wakan*, the sacred road.

Now in Canada, they continued up Frenchmen's Creek, which the Canadian maps labeled the White Mud Creek. About sixty miles farther, they reached a headland called Pinto Horse Butte. Watered by the White Mud, which rose in the timbered Cypress Hills to the west, Pinto Horse Butte rested on the northwestern end of Wood Mountain. It afforded a good place to camp without worrying about Bear Coat.

The people had rested a few days when lookouts sighted seven mounted men approaching the village. Some wore scarlet coats and white helmets. They boldly advanced, seemingly unafraid of the Indians, dismounted, and walked toward the tipis. The Lakota lookouts had been circling the party long enough to bring word to the village of the intruders. Who they were remained to be learned.

2

James Morrow Walsh

The small group of men who rode to Pinto Horse Butte on that spring day in 1877 were Queen Victoria's representatives in the Canadian West. The leader was Maj. James M. Walsh of the North-West Mounted Police, the constabulary recently established to bring law and order to Canada's newly acquired North-West Territory.

The world into which James Walsh was born changed dramatically during his lifetime. He changed with it, grasping the opportunities it afforded. From the Atlantic to the Pacific, the country north of the boundary with the United States had long been a part of the British Empire.

Walsh was born in 1840 in Prescott, a small town on the north bank of the St. Lawrence River in the British colony of Upper Canada (present-day Ontario), which a year after his birth united with Lower Canada (present-day Quebec) to take the name of Canada. The colonial capital, Ottawa, lay forty miles north of Prescott.

The Walsh progeny numbered three girls and six boys. James was the oldest. In the local classrooms he proved deficient in academics but superior in athletics. He worked a variety of jobs in Prescott but increasingly aspired to a military career. At twenty he was captain of the Prescott Fire Brigade and in 1862 was studying in the Kingston Military School, which would later become the Royal Military Academy. Kingston lay sixty miles upstream from Prescott, where the St. Lawrence River formed from the outflow of Lake Ontario. Walsh gained a brief exposure to military life in 1866, when the Fenians, the Irish liberation movement, launched raids into Canada from the United States. Walsh served as a lieutenant in the Prescott Rifles and later as captain in a battalion of volunteer militia. Most of the fighting, however, took place farther to the east.

Walsh continued his military training at the Toronto Cavalry School, from which he graduated in 1869. The commandant of the school wrote of him: "He is the smartest and most efficient officer that has yet passed through the Cavalry School. He is a good rider and particularly quick and confident at drill." Later in 1869 he emerged with distinction from the Toronto School of Gunnery.

Of Walsh in this formative period, his biographer wrote: "Walsh's ideals reflected his rural Ontario upbringing and military training. He had fine posture, a proud bearing, and was a trim, muscular, agile, five foot nine inches in height, with intense dark eyes. He was an active, confident, forceful, decisive and impatient personality. Brave, ambitious and daring, he was also vain, flamboyant and capable of much bravado."[1]

Walsh proved a reliable and efficient officer, and also flamboyant like the American Custer. A newsman penned a description of Walsh:

He is a very handsome young fellow, straight, slim, with an eye like a hawk and an iron frame, conscious of his good looks and thirsting for display and adventure. A born leader of men, with much decision and shrewdness and a showy way of doing things, it is not to be wondered that he has already made his mark in the Northwest and acquired singular influence over the Indians.[2]

Still another newsman added to the portrait:

His parents were born in Ireland, and, in his temperament, Walsh is a thoroughbred Irishman. He is quick, nervous, vivacious, intense in his application where his interest is aroused, generous in his dealings, and his experience with the Indians proves his courage He has a perfect admiration for the character of the Lakotas and believes them to be superior to any Indians extant. And they, in return, have a wonderful affection for him. They are completely under his control; and I am told by those who are engaged in business at Wood Mountain, that his influence over Sitting Bull and the Chiefs of the tribe is perfect. Walsh brought them to terms, he says, by persuasion, but really by the force of his will.[3]

In 1870, while managing a hotel in Prescott, Walsh wed Mary Mowat of Brockville, fifteen miles up the St. Lawrence from Prescott. Six months later Mary gave birth to a daughter, Cora.

In the thirty years since his birth, Walsh had observed a series of momentous changes in his homeland. The guiding figure in these changes was Sir John A. Macdonald. First a legislator, then in 1857 premier of Canada, Macdonald crafted a coalition of parties that met in London to establish a nation. In 1867 the parliament of the United Kingdom passed the British North America Act. It created the Dominion of Canada, consisting of the provinces of Ontario, Quebec, New Brunswick, and Nova Scotia, with more to follow. Each province would have its own government, with a federal government presiding from Ottawa. Each would have a house of commons and a senate, with the Crown's interests represented by a British lieutenant governor. Sir John Macdonald was elected prime minister and served, with a five-year interruption, until his death in 1891.

Macdonald intended to make the new dominion a great nation extending west to the Pacific Ocean, bound together by a transcontinental railroad. That required gaining hegemony over British Columbia, the Crown's colony on the Pacific Coast, and the vast wilderness in between, Rupert's Land. The latter had been the fiefdom of the Hudson's Bay Company for two centuries. In 1869 the Crown repossessed Rupert's Land and in 1870 sold it and the huge territory north of it to the Dominion of Canada for £300,000. It was named the North-West Territory. British Columbia joined the federation in 1871, with its capital in Victoria. Macdonald's Canada had become a continental nation. In the same year, a revolt of mixed-blood Métis on Red River prompted a British-Canadian military campaign that ended the uprising with a compromise in the Manitoba Act, which cemented the province of Manitoba into Macdonald's dominion, its capital at Winnipeg.

As early as 1869, the prime minister began planning for a force to establish law and order in the new lands. Throughout the British Empire, the Royal Irish Constabulary had provided the model for frontier forces. Such a formation appeared the ideal way to bring the Queen's law to the Indian tribes of the plains and mountains and the settlers expected to trek west. It also was intended to aid the projected transcontinental railway and, more immediately, to rid the West of the whiskey peddlers from Montana. The force's particular distinction was to combine both police and judicial functions in one outfit. Members could arrest malefactors, then try them and adjudicate their punishment. Military training buttressed their law-enforcement function.

Not until May 1873 did Prime Minister Macdonald overcome delays and win the Crown's approval for the North-West Mounted Police. He and his cabinet drew up plans to design and man the force. It was to number three hundred men divided into six divisions of fifty men each. They would wear scarlet uniforms to emphasize for the Indians the distinction between American soldiers and Canadian police. Among the first nine senior officers chosen by Macdonald was James M. Walsh. He ranked as inspector, a title shortly changed to superintendent, but throughout his career, in common with other officers, he clung to his militia title of major. "This is an opportunity for a man to do something great," he declared with typical bravado, "and I am going to do it."

Something great began with the "March West," a defining event celebrated in the lore of the Mounted Police ever after. On July 8, 1874, Commissioner George A. French and his assistant commissioner, James F. Macleod, led the North-West Mounted Police out of Fort Dufferin and set forth into the "Great Lone Land," the vast wilderness extending from the Red River on the east to the Rocky Mountains, a thousand miles to the west. Inspector Walsh commanded D Division, one of the six fifty-man units garbed in scarlet tunics and white helmets. Following the 275 troopers were a supply train of 114 two-wheeled carts, a herd of 93 beef cattle, and assorted other conveyances.[4]

Heroic as many accounts portray the March West, it was a bruising ordeal for men and horses. Storms, droughts, disease, dwindling rations and forage, rough country, exhausted men, dying horses, stampeding cattle, and other setbacks marred the tortuous course of the march. Despite the adversities, the expedition reached its destination in late September 1874, without a single death. Here, on the Old Man River, fifty miles south of Calgary and one hundred miles north of the international boundary, Assistant Commissioner Macleod erected Fort Macleod. He soon replaced French as commissioner.

The North-West Mounted Police may have overplayed the drama of their March West, but in succeeding years they lived up to the role set for them. Although much of the popular story was doubtless apocryphal, it illustrated the élan of the force.

Throughout winter 1874–75, Major Walsh demonstrated his efficiency by undertaking special assignments for Colonel Macleod throughout the Mounted Police domain. In spring 1875 Macleod dispatched Walsh to the Cypress Hills, a ragged outcropping in the prairie two hundred miles east of Fort Macleod. Here he erected Fort Walsh, destined to become the most important post in the West, and in 1878 the headquarters of the North-West Mounted Police. Two years later a newspaper correspondent described Fort Walsh as

> an irregular stockade of upright logs, inclosing all the offices and buildings, which are likewise built of logs, necessary for the accommodation of a garrison. Whitewashed on every part except its roof, the fort nestles like a wild swan . . . between the surrounding heights. A scraggly but picturesque little settlement adjoins it.[5]

Major Walsh had a huge domain to cover from Fort Walsh. For his first year, he busied himself suppressing the whiskey trade, making friends with local Indians, and building a road from the fort to the Montana town of Fort Benton. This was a steamboat landing on the Missouri River from which the police drew supplies and kept in telegraphic contact with Ottawa. This necessity was caused by the portion of the Canadian Shield, a massive geological formation, that thrust above the earth's surface in the area of the Red River of the North and blocked east-west transportation. Until the railroad breached the barrier, the Mounted Police had to travel though the United States to reach their western stations.

In May 1876, with hostilities between the U.S. Army and the Lakota Indians roiling the American side of the boundary, the Lakotas commanded the government's attention. Apprehension that "hostile" Lakotas might seek refuge in Canada and use it as a base from which to continue the war across the border into Montana worried Ottawa. Fort Macleod and Fort Walsh each received an infusion of one hundred troopers to strengthen the frontier. After George Custer was overwhelmed on the Little Bighorn on June 25, 1876, the government took alarm.[6]

Major Walsh had contracted erysipelas, an outer skin infection, and had gone to Hot Springs, Arkansas, for treatment. A telegram from Ottawa informed him of the Custer disaster and ordered him back to Fort Walsh as soon as possible. He arrived on August 1, 1876, and promptly sent scouts to keep watch on the international boundary southeast of Fort Walsh.[7]

Early in December 1876 Walsh's scouts reported Lakotas camped at Wood Mountain, 120 miles east of Fort Walsh. This landmark was a plateau of flat-topped hills scored by timbered coulees rising fourteen hundred feet above the surrounding plain and extending one hundred miles from west to east. The international boundary lay only twenty miles to the south. Walsh had already received instructions from Colonel Macleod to confront any such Lakota refugees, explain the Queen's Law, and prohibit traders from providing them with arms and ammunition. In his year working out of Fort Walsh, the major had dealt often enough with the local tribes—Cree, Assiniboine, Piegan, Blood, Santee Sioux, and above all Blackfeet—to feel comfortable relating to these people. Therefore, he expertly dealt with the first Lakotas to cross the border: Black Moon and his people in December 1876 and Four Horns and his followers in March 1877.

En route back to Fort Walsh after meeting Four Horns, Walsh established "lookout posts" at Wood Mountain and the eastern end of Cypress Hills. At each place he left one constable and two sub-constables. The two stations would soon become permanent: Wood Mountain Post and East End Post.

By spring 1877 Major Walsh had dealt twice with refugee Lakotas—with Black Moon and Four Horns and their followers. He had grown skilled in the delicate process and appeared to have been successful in both instances. To the Americans, however, Sitting Bull was the archvillain, and he remained south of the boundary. His crossing appeared almost certain to happen soon.

Police commissioner James Macleod had journeyed to Ottawa to express his concern to Prime Minister Alexander Mackenzie, who had replaced Macdonald in 1874. The Lakotas were upsetting the resident Blackfeet, Crees, and other Indians, he advised. Although they had made many promises, Macleod had little faith in them. He believed that efforts should be made at once to get these Indians back across the boundary. The longer delayed, the harder to accomplish. The commissioner recommended to the prime minister that communication be opened with the United States to learn on what conditions the Lakotas would be received. He thought the Americans would be pleased to get them back because their proximity to the border caused anxiety and trouble.[8]

Macleod was wrong on two counts. The U.S. government did not want them back, and the Lakotas did not want to go back. In fact, Walsh and the police were not trying to get them to go back.

At Fort Walsh Major Walsh remained alert to confront the most powerful Lakota chief of all, the redoubtable Sitting Bull. After returning to the fort following his council with Four Horns, Walsh learned from a scout that Four Horns's people were moving north along the White Mud Creek toward Pinto Horse Butte, a rugged outcropping on the northwestern flank of Wood Mountain. Two weeks later another report arrived. Sitting Bull was south of the boundary moving north. Walsh intended to greet him when he arrived. On May 8, with scouts Louis Léveillé and Gabriel Solomon, Sergeant George Rolph, and three constables, he rode east, intending to make camp near the White Mud and wait for the chief. Other scouts ranged widely in advance.[9]

A two-day journey brought the little outfit to the White Mud. Here they discovered the remnants of a large village, suggesting that Sitting Bull had already arrived. The trail pointed farther north. Preceded by scouts, the police followed the trail until night fell, then continued the next day. As they advanced, their scouts discovered mounted Indians appearing on the surrounding hills, and in growing numbers they circled the patrol warily. In this hilly country their village remained hidden until Walsh and his team almost rode into it. They dismounted to confront Sitting Bull.

Sitting Bull and 135 lodges had raised their tipis at Pinto Horse Butte and had rested a few days when lookouts sighted seven mounted men approaching from the south. Some wore scarlet tunics and white helmets. They boldly advanced, apparently unafraid. The Lakota lookouts had been circling the party long enough to bring word to Sitting Bull's lodge. Ever sensitive to danger from white men, he dispatched the charismatic young Sans Arc chief Spotted Eagle to face these men at the village edge.

Backed by an array of chiefs and headmen, Spotted Eagle warily confronted the strangers. Confidently they advanced, and Spotted Eagle shook hands with the man who seemed to be the leader. A round of handshaking relaxed the atmosphere. Another of the white men interpreted Spotted Eagle's words. These white men had entered the camp of Sitting Bull, he said, and never had white men been so bold as to invade this sanctuary, thus putting their lives at risk. The white leader was Maj. James M. Walsh of the North-West Mounted Police, and he remembered Spotted Eagle as "the finest speaker in the Lakota camp [with] a most wonderful flow of language and a powerful voice." Leaving his comrades to confront the white men, Spotted Eagle went back into the village and informed

Sitting Bull of the situation. He joined Spotted Eagle and a group of other waiting chiefs and ventured out to meet the white men. One of the whites extended his hand and Sitting Bull shook it, then shook hands all around.[10]

Even though it was already about five o'clock in the afternoon, Spotted Eagle called for a council. In a hastily erected lodge of large dimensions, the chiefs and headmen arranged themselves in a circle. Sitting Bull entered last and seated himself in the space reserved for the head chief. With scout Louis Léveillé and interpreter Gabriel Solomon at his side, Walsh sat in the center of the circle.

Walsh stood, along with Léveillé and Solomon, and addressed the assembled chiefs. He had come, he said, to meet with the newcomers and explain the rules they had to live by if they intended to stay in Canada. Sitting Bull got to his feet and walked forward to shake hands with Walsh. He then launched into a long tirade on the iniquities of the Americans, how they had murdered his women and children, how they had chased him and his people "like hungry wolves seeking for my blood." He and his people had crossed the line looking for peace. The "grass in Canada is not stained by blood," he declared, and they wanted only to rest and be free of war. He hoped that Canada would deal gently with them. Spotted Eagle and other chiefs made their own speeches, essentially echoing Sitting Bull's.

Walsh then said what he had come to say.

Did Sitting Bull know he was in the White Mother's country? Yes, he replied.

Why did he come? He and his people had been driven from their homes by the Americans, and they came in peace.

Did he intend to stay here just for the winter and in the spring cross the boundary and resume the war? No, he wanted to remain and wanted Walsh to ask the White Mother to take pity on him.

Walsh next gave a simple description of the White Mother's laws and again stressed that they must be obeyed. (The offenses were typical of most jurisdictions, e.g., murder, theft, resisting arrest; the rules were applied specifically to the Indians and were designed to maintain order and obedience to the law.)

After Walsh finished, each of the chiefs rose to deliver a formal speech. The theme of each was to ask that that the Queen take pity on them and let them remain.

Walsh concluded the council by declaring that the White Mother would never allow them to cross the boundary and make war on the Americans, then return to enjoy her protection. If they intended that, they should go back home now and stay there.

Sitting Bull readily agreed to all the requirements set forth by Walsh. He followed that with fine words about how wonderful he now felt, how much he trusted the redcoats and respected the White Mother. On the other side of the line he had been fighting because he had to. But now he had buried his weapons and would do no wrong in the land of the White Mother. If any of his men went back across the line, they would not be allowed to return. His heart was now good.

Sitting Bull's oratory impressed Walsh, although he was shrewd enough to understand that the chief's hatred of "Long Knives" might lead him to forget some of his promises.

The next morning, as the police packed to leave, Sitting Bull witnessed a spectacle that demonstrated how the redcoats dealt with malefactors. Three Indians rode up leading five horses. Interpreter Solomon identified them for Walsh as Assiniboines from the Missouri River, one of whom was White Dog, an infamous warrior well known throughout the Plains country. Solomon also observed that he thought three of the horses belonged to a Catholic priest in the Cypress Hills. Walsh directed Solomon and Léveillé to inspect the horses. The two examined the animals closely and returned to report them stolen. Walsh then instructed Sergeant Rolph to arrest White Dog and the other Assiniboines. They were standing near several dozen curious Lakota warriors. McCutcheon and two constables walked over to White Dog and told him that he was under arrest. Why? demanded the Assiniboine. For possessing horses that did not belong to him, replied the sergeant. White Dog angrily protested and declared that the horses were his and he would not be arrested. Walsh approached to confront White Dog, who clearly expected the Lakotas to take his side. The scouts rounded up the horses and brought them to Walsh. Placing his hand on White Dog's shoulder, he said, "You say you will neither be arrested nor surrender these horses. I arrest you, and [pointing to each of the other Assiniboines] you, and you, and you, and you." Lakota warriors anxiously watched the drama but made no move. White Dog believed that these friends would come to his aid and fight off the redcoats, but they simply watched. Walsh ordered the third constable to bring over a set of leg irons. He then instructed White Dog to explain where and how he obtained the horses and what he intended to do with them or he would put the irons on him and take him to his headquarters at Fort Walsh. White Dog sagged when he saw that Lakota warriors would not rescue him. He had found the horses wandering loose on the prairie, he explained, and he did not know that it was a crime to take them. To defuse the confrontation, Walsh merely ordered White Dog never again to molest property north of the line.

As White Dog turned to go, he muttered some words in a threatening manner. Walsh stopped him and ordered him to repeat what he had said through the interpreter. When White Dog resisted, Walsh told him to repeat the words or be taken to Fort Walsh. White Dog simply stammered that he had not meant them as a threat.

For Sitting Bull and the Lakotas, Walsh had staged a telling drama of the White Mother's laws and the manner in which her redcoats would enforce them. It was a lesson not soon forgotten.[11]

The lesson impressed Sitting Bull so much that, just as Walsh and his party were about to depart, the chief asked him to come to his lodge and explain again the rules he and his people must obey. That request signaled to Walsh that the White Dog incident had succeeded in its purpose. This first meeting of Sitting Bull and Walsh left each with a dawning admiration and respect for the other. Later, as the Lakotas became more familiar with the police, they called Walsh "Long Lance" because the police had a ceremonial unit in which the men carried lances tipped with forked red-and-white pennants.

Sitting Bull proved his new loyalty almost immediately. On May 26, 1877, word reached him of a party of horsemen riding up the White Mud toward the village. With a contingent of warriors, he

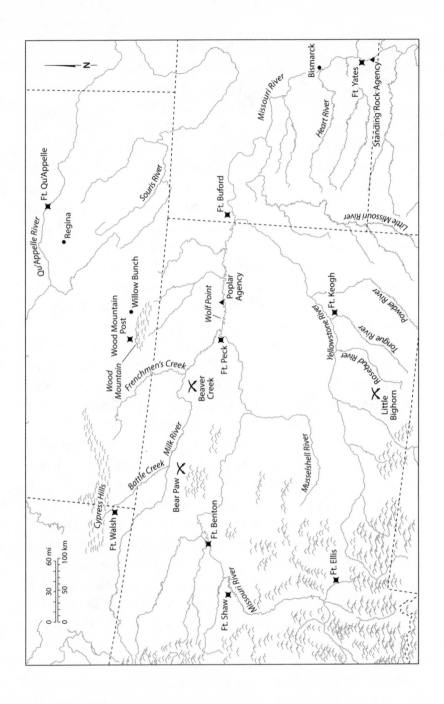

Map 2. Sitting Bull, the Canadian Years, 1877–1881. Bill Nelson Cartography.

rode to meet the newcomers. They were a Catholic priest, Rev. Martin Marty, two other white men, and eight Lakota Indian guides. One of the white men, John Howard, was chief scout for Bear Coat Miles, and the other was an interpreter. The Black Robe had journeyed from Standing Rock Agency to find Sitting Bull, then thought to be in Montana, and try to persuade him to surrender and go to the agency. The priest described his welcome by Sitting Bull as warm and friendly, but that seems doubtful as they were promptly taken to the village and confined. Had they appeared three weeks earlier, the priest's companions would probably be dead and the priest himself in danger. Now, however, Sitting Bull intended to comply with Walsh's insistence that, if any strangers entered his village, he should at once be informed. The chief dispatched his able nephew, One Bull, and two others to Fort Walsh to carry the message.[12]

They reached the fort on May 29, the same day the assistant commissioner of the force, Lt. Col. Acheson G. Irvine, arrived from Fort Benton on his way to Ottawa. He delayed his journey so that he could take charge of the response to One Bull's message. Two days later a delegation set forth for Sitting Bull's village. It consisted of Colonel Irvine, Major Walsh, two subinspectors, and an escort of constables. They reached their destination on June 2 and had scarcely dismounted when Sitting Bull and other chiefs walked down and shook hands with the officers. Irvine recalled that

I was particularly struck with Sitting Bull. He is a man of somewhat short stature, but with a pleasant face, a mouth showing great determination, and a fine high forehead. When he smiled, as he often did, his face brightened up wonderfully. I should say he is a man of about forty-five years of age [forty-six].[13]

An hour later Sitting Bull escorted the group to an immense council lodge that had just been erected. It consisted of tipi poles with buffalo skins drawn around them set to form two cone-shaped spaces merged into one. Flaps at the front were drawn aside and the police seated on buffalo robes spread across the opening. They faced the prominent chiefs. About one hundred men, women, and children filed in and sat in the space behind and to the side of the chiefs. Father Marty and his two companions remained elsewhere in the village.[14]

Major Walsh rose and, addressing Sitting Bull and the other chiefs, stated that Colonel Irvine was the White Mother's highest chief in the country (Colonel Macleod was in Ottawa) and that he had come to hear what the chiefs had to say and to learn why they had come to Canada.

To open the council, Pretty Bear stood and delivered a long prayer, mostly addressed to the White Mother. Nearing the conclusion, he raised a peace pipe and, using a glowing buffalo chip, lit the pipe, then yielded it to Sitting Bull, who pointed it in four directions, took a puff, and had each officer smoke. Sitting Bull emptied the pipe and buried the ashes, then broke the pipe into four pieces and laid them over the spot—a ceremony that intrigued Irvine.

Next Sitting Bull spoke, partly an oration on the evils that had driven him north, partly prayer to the White Mother, imploring her to allow the Lakotas to live in Canada. Adjutant Clark duly recorded what he and the interpreter could understand, but it was difficult for the white men to make sense of some of the speech. Sitting Bull finished by alluding to the three whites in the village. "The Americans who came here asked me if I threw our land away. I told him God [doubtless Wakantanka] did not tell me to. Crazy Horse is still holding it. He is looking at me to see if it is good here." Then he ended his oration: "I am through."

Sweet Bird, Spotted Eagle, Pretty Bear, and Sitting Bull again followed the opening speech. They repeated the same theme: why they were in Canada and their hope that the White Mother would treat them well.

Colonel Irvine addressed the chiefs with words they had heard before but that were nonetheless reassuring:

You are in the Queen's, the Great Mother's country. Major Walsh has explained the law of the land which belongs to the Great White Mother. As long as you remain in the land of the Great White

Mother, you must obey her laws. As long as you behave yourselves you have nothing to fear. The Great White Mother, the Queen, takes care of everyone in her land in every part of the world.

Now that you are in the Queen's land, you must not cross the line to fight the Americans and return to this country. . . .

In the Queen's land we all live like one family. If a white man or Indian does wrong she will get them punished. The Queen's arm is very strong. . . . If anyone comes into your camp like those Americans did, come to the fort and tell Major Walsh about these men. As soon as your young men arrived at the fort, we started, and I came here to see you and shake your hand. . . . You need not be alarmed. The Americans cannot cross the line after you. You and your families can sleep sound and not be afraid.

At the conclusion of the council, Colonel Irvine went to talk with the three Americans. Father Marty told him he had come simply to try to persuade Sitting Bull to journey to the agency and accept the government's terms. Howard said he had been sent by Miles to ask Walsh if Sitting Bull intended to return.

Sitting Bull asked for another council in the afternoon, with the priest attending. After Pretty Bear's prayer and the peace-pipe ritual, Sitting Bull addressed a long speech to Father Marty, repeating the usual motivations for his flight to Canada. Marty had sensed the outcome when he first talked to Sitting Bull, and now he simply offered to accompany the Lakotas back to their agency if they wanted to go (Sitting Bull had never lived at this or any agency). He even said he believed Sitting Bull would be better off if he remained in Canada.

Spotted Eagle intervened to ask if the Long Knives had sent the priest. "I am not sent here by the government," Marty responded, "but I am assured that what I promise you will be carried out. Do you intend to return to the other side or remain?" Sitting Bull turned to Irvine. "If I remain here will you protect me?" "I told you the White Mother would," replied Irvine, "as long as you behave yourself." Ending the exchange, Sitting Bull delivered his emphatic decision:

"What would I return for? To have my horses and arms taken away? What have the Americans to give me? They have no lands. Once I was rich, plenty of money, but the Americans stole it all in the Black Hills. I have come to remain with the White Mother's children."

The police spent the night at the village before leaving the next morning. The day's proceedings elated Colonel Irvine. Sitting Bull had impressed him as an eloquent patriot, and he felt that he had made a friend of Sitting Bull, who would live up to his promises. The interpreter informed Irvine that this was the happiest night the Lakota village had passed in many months. Irvine himself said he had never seen a happier lot of people. A final surprise inflated the colonel's euphoria. At about 11:30 that night Sitting Bull and the interpreter quietly slipped into Irvine's tent. "He sat on my bed until an early hour of the morning," Irvine recalled, "telling me in a subdued tone his many grievances against the 'Long Knives.'"

The meeting of June 2, 1877, was highly successful from the viewpoint both of Sitting Bull and the police officer. Sitting Bull had gained emphatic promises from the White Mother's highest chief in the Indian country that he could live here in peace with the assurance that the Long Knives could not harm him. The only condition was that he obey the White Mother's laws. Colonel Irvine had repeated the terms on which Sitting Bull could remain and departed with the conviction that the terms would be met by the chief. If either worried that the terms might be difficult to meet, neither betrayed it.

Although Sitting Bull had readily responded to the authority of the officer, Colonel Irvine had not replaced Major Walsh in his affections. Irvine was merely passing through. Walsh remained, and he was the one who spoke for the redcoats. Sitting Bull knew that Walsh was the man he would have to deal with.

When Major Walsh met Sitting Bull in spring 1877, he was not a fledgling at the craft of Lakota diplomacy. In December 1876 he had greeted Black Moon and his people, and in March 1877 he had met with Four Horns and his people. To both he had recited the same message: obey the laws and rules of the White Mother and never cross the boundary back into the United States. Both chiefs, like

Sitting Bull in May 1877, had promised to comply with the conditions for remaining in Canada. Although retaining their customary independence, these chiefs acknowledged Sitting Bull's primacy and became part of his following.

The summer of 1877 placed little stress on Sitting Bull. The buffalo had not yet begun their precipitous decline, so hunger was not a pressing issue. Jean Luis Legaré's trading post at Wood Mountain welcomed the Lakotas, treating them fairly and favorably. And the meeting with Colonel Irvine had reinforced Major Walsh's assurances of a home in Canada. Walsh frequently came for a friendly visit.

Behind the scenes, however, another story was taking shape. Colonel Irvine's fine words did not reflect Canadian policy. Ottawa quickly set him straight. Reacting to Irvine's report of June 6 on the meeting with Sitting Bull, the secretary of state informed Irvine that the Lakotas should not be allowed to believe that they could take permanent residence in Canada. They could be assured of temporary protection, but the final policy would rest with the government in Ottawa.

The government had already decided. On June 20 the British chargé d'affaires in Washington, Frederick R. Plunkett, transmitted to the American secretary of state a report of the Canadian Privy Council requesting the United States to use its best endeavors to persuade the Lakotas to return to America. In foreign affairs London handled all matters for the Dominion, which complicated diplomacy. The Privy Council had acted on the recommendation of Colonel Macleod, who clearly saw the troubles the presence of the Lakotas would stir.[15]

In Washington the State Department referred the British communication to the War Department for comment. That fell to Gen. William T. Sherman, who, accompanied by Gen. Alfred H. Terry, was visiting Colonel Miles's cantonment on the Yellowstone at the mouth of the Tongue. With characteristic bluntness Sherman gave his views, as concurred in by Terry. "We agree," he wrote, "that the English authorities should *now* elect to adopt these refugee Indians as their own, or force them back to our side of the line before they recuperate their ponies and collect new supplies of ammunition." If they were allowed to use Canada as a base of operations against the United States, "the act will surely be equivalent to an act of hostility, which I am sure the English authorities do not intend." Sherman recommended that a commission composed of both American and Canadian officials meet with the Lakotas and offer to conduct them back to their agencies.[16]

Sherman did not need to know about the Mounted Police councils with the Lakotas to understand that such a commission would probably accomplish nothing substantive, but would end as a gesture to demonstrate that the Americans took the issue seriously.

Ottawa grew increasingly impatient with the slow pace of negotiations in Washington. Not only did the U.S. State Department delay the process, but the necessity of relying on the British colonial office to handle relations with the Americans consumed much time. Chargé Plunkett dealt with the State Department, and all his dispatches had to be routed through London, as did dispatches from Ottawa to Washington. In August Prime Minister Alexander Mackenzie decided on a direct approach, sending Interior Minister David Mills to Washington to join with Plunkett in pushing for a solution. On August 8, 1877, the two took the issue to Secretary of the Interior Carl Schurz. The secretary at once escorted them to the Executive Mansion to meet Pres. Rutherford B. Hayes, who directed that the two men and Secretary of War George McCrary gather in his office the next day to resolve the problem.

They gathered, but the problem proved difficult to resolve. Secretary Schurz forcefully contended that Canada had an obligation to disarm the Indians and send them back across the border—the same stance General Sherman had advocated. Mills tried to explain that the Mounted Police were not strong enough to do this. When Schurz persisted, Mills countered that perhaps the Americans could make a generous offer that would induce the chiefs to return. The president decided that a commission should be formed to journey to Canada for this purpose, but with the caveat that, if the Indians came back, they had to give up their arms.

The president named Brig. Gen. Alfred H. Terry to chair the Sitting Bull Commission, and Terry persuaded a wartime comrade, one-armed former general A. G. Lawrence, to serve as the second commissioner. As secretary, the president assigned his military aide, Capt. (and brevet lieutenant colonel) Henry C. Corbin. Terry took with him his own aide, Capt. Edward W. Smith. Accompanying the commission were a stenographer and interpreter and two first-rate newsmen, Jerome Stillson of the *New York Herald* and Charles Diehl of the *Chicago Times*.[17]

Terry was hardly the most appropriate chairman. As commanding general of the Department of Dakota, he had served as Custer's immediate superior in the campaign that led to Custer's death. Of all the American generals, he was least likely to establish rapport with Sitting Bull. The Canadian officers sensed this from the beginning and had little hope for a favorable outcome. Yet at least the Americans were finally paying attention to the issue.

The commission gathered on September 11, 1877, at General Terry's headquarters in St. Paul, Minnesota, and three days later embarked westward by railway. A thousand-mile journey, by both rail and horse, brought them to the boundary on October 14. Here they were met by Colonel Macleod and an escort clad in scarlet tunics and white helmets and bearing lances tipped with red-and-white pennants. They rode into Fort Walsh two days later.[18]

3

The Sitting Bull Commission

Major Walsh and Colonel Irvine had made the Lakotas feel welcome and safe from any threat of the Long Knives. The rules were simple. Abiding by them meant they could make new homes in the realm of the White Mother. The chiefs placed no qualification on their promises to the police officers. As Sitting Bull had asked Father Marty, *why* would they go back across the medicine line when they knew the Long Knives would chase and kill them? *Why* would they surrender when they knew their guns and horses would be taken from them and they would be restricted to their agencies? Sitting Bull, Four Horns, Black Moon, and other chiefs had not reached exalted rank in their tribes without a deep understanding of their people. They understood that the young men valued their independence and would exercise it when they wished even though the chiefs disapproved. They understood that they themselves would take whatever action they believed necessary for the welfare of their people, including punishing or excusing errant young men. For the chiefs, the policy now was to settle in Canada and carry out their promises to the redcoats. For the young men, exercising their customary independence could bring trouble to the chiefs and all their people. But they broke the rules anyway.

One such instance, reported by the U.S. consul at Winnipeg, occurred on June 23, 1877, near Wood Mountain:

> Four traders from Winnipeg . . . were surrounded by a war party of 27 Sioux and urged to trade powder and ball for horses branded

U.S. They declined, whereupon the Indians used force and robbed the traders of three kegs of powder and a bag of balls. No Canadian force is adequate to prevent or punish such outrages.[1]

Such tribal complexities undoubtedly disturbed Sitting Bull and threatened his relationship with Major Walsh. Even so, whenever pressed by either Americans or Canadians, the answer was a resounding *no*. Sitting Bull and his fellow chiefs would not go back. They hated the Americans, and they had found a land where the white man was trustworthy. Here they could remain free if they obeyed the rules, and they had been welcomed by kindly redcoats.

Moreover, no one would go back because they were bound by a compact. No family belonged to the camp without the permission of a council, and no family left the camp without a council's permission. Any who violated the compact faced punishment by the *akicita*, the tribal police commanded by One Bull. Retribution, or "soldiering," could take many forms, such as physical harm or destruction of personal property. Sitting Bull had imposed this mandate to ensure that no one deserted to surrender south of the boundary, and to disobey it not only courted severe consequence but defied the powerful head chief.[2]

Throughout summer 1877 Major Walsh occasionally rode from Wood Mountain Post to nearby Pinto Horse Butte to visit Sitting Bull. Despite unruly young men, they got along well. Sitting Bull began to slip into a mode of following up on everything that Walsh suggested. A solid relationship was developing. Walsh was becoming the only white man the legendarily resistant Sitting Bull ever trusted.

The strength of the relationship was soon put to the test. Unknown to Sitting Bull, the issue of Lakotas in Canada was a subject of diplomatic negotiations between Canada and the United States in Washington DC. The two sides produced a solution of sorts in September 1877. The U.S. commission to treat with Sitting Bull, headed by Brig. Gen. Alfred H. Terry, reached the boundary south of Fort Walsh on October 14, 1877.

Walsh had been in Fort Walsh when a telegram from the Canadian secretary of state, dated October 1, directed him to persuade Sitting Bull to come to Fort Walsh and meet with the commission. Walsh left Fort Walsh on the same day and reached Wood Mountain on the seventh. He at once called a council of Sitting Bull and his fellow chiefs and announced that the White Mother would be very glad if they would accompany him to Fort Walsh and meet with the American commissioners. The instant answer from Sitting Bull was NO. It would make their hearts feel bad to meet with any Americans, they said. Americans had lied to them so often that they could not believe them. The Lakotas wanted to remain in the White Mother's country.[3]

Walsh had learned how to deal with Sitting Bull, however. Laboring all day, frequently citing the Queen's wishes, he finally overcame Sitting Bull's resistance. He would do as Long Lance wished, testimony to how close the two had grown since their first meeting five months earlier. He agreed to go if they could postpone departure until the next day, October 8.

The Lakotas were ready the next morning, but events intruded. The Nez Perce's conflict with the U.S. Army had moved from the tribe's Idaho homeland across the Rocky Mountains into Montana. Here the Nez Perces had hoped to find succor with the Crows, but the Crows were allied with the U.S. Army. The Nez Perces then fell back to their alternate resolve: seek refuge with Sitting Bull in Canada. By mid-September they were moving north toward the Missouri River and ultimately Canada.

When the Lakotas learned of the Nez Perce advance, young men painted themselves and made ready to cross the boundary to aid them, even though the two tribes had never been friendly. Major Walsh also tried to restrain his charges. Repeatedly he emphasized that the Mounted Police would not let any Lakotas who crossed the border to help the Nez Perces come back. The condition for living in Canada had been made clear to them, and any violation would be decisively dealt with by the White Mother.[4]

Sitting Bull had promised to begin the journey to Fort Walsh the next morning, October 8. At midmorning, however, he asked for a delay. Some of his scouts were out, and he wanted to wait until they returned. Walsh gave his consent, but at that moment one of the scouts rode up with word that a large party of horsemen was approaching from the south. Another quickly arrived to report that they were whites. Pandemonium erupted in the village. The women began to dismantle the tipis and pack in preparation for flight. The men gathered their horses and made ready to ride south. Walsh tried to quell the turmoil. He said he would go himself and find out who they were. That held most back, but two hundred warriors followed.

When Walsh met the newcomers, they proved not to be whites but Nez Perces, fifty men, forty women, and many children, together with three hundred horses. The group was badly shot up, men, women, and children bleeding from bullet wounds in arms, legs, and body. Unknown to Walsh, these were people led by White Bird, a Nez Perce war chief who had escaped the battle and siege of Bear Paw, September 30 to October 5. Col. Nelson A. Miles had cut off the flight of the Nez Perces and in the costly conflict at Bear Paw forced the rest to surrender. Gen. Oliver Howard, who had led the pursuit from Idaho, reached the scene as Chief Joseph made an eloquent surrender speech. These Nez Perces were to remain in Canada, interacting with Sitting Bull's people.[5]

Sitting Bull's party numbered thirty chiefs and headmen, including Spotted Eagle, Bear's Head, Flying Bird, Iron Dog, Little Knife, and Crow. The rest of the people remained behind. On October 8 Walsh's party had been packed and ready to leave for Fort Walsh when the bloodied Nez Perces arrived. Their presence afforded Sitting Bull another chance to say no to Walsh. He convened another council and addressed harsh words to Long Lance: "Why do you come and seek us to go and talk with men who are killing our own race? You see these men, women, and children, wounded and bleeding, we cannot talk with men who have blood on their hands. They have stained the grass of the White Mother with it." Walsh could only reply that he had been ordered by Colonel Macleod to bring Sitting Bull and his chiefs to Fort Walsh to talk with the Americans. They need not accept any offers from them, Walsh added, if they did not want to. But if they refused this request of the White Mother, they would be the first people to do such a thing. The chiefs talked quietly among themselves for several minutes. Then Sitting Bull told Walsh they would go, but he wanted to wait until the next morning. Walsh agreed.[6]

Again, on October 9, Sitting Bull stalled the departure by calling another council. In this one, all the anxieties of the past boiled over. Walsh had dealt with them repeatedly, but once more he had to persuade the Lakotas that they must do as the White Mother wished. Sitting Bull finally understood that he had no choice: the White Mother and Major Walsh had insisted, and in their new homes that prevailed. At last, at eleven o'clock in the morning, the procession got underway.

That afternoon, at the eastern end of the Cypress Hills, they met Colonel Macleod. He learned from Walsh that the morning council had not been entirely decisive. The chiefs had slowed the march by constantly stopping to smoke and reconsider their grudging consent to meet the Americans. The wounded Nez Perces still affected them badly. Despite Walsh's repeated promises, the chiefs could not shake the fear that the American soldiers would cross the line and attack them. Before departure the next morning Macleod met with the chiefs in an effort to dispel their dread. He gave the same pledge that so often had been made since the Lakotas came to Canada: if the Americans crossed the line, a wall would confront them that they dared not cross. If they did, the redcoats would side with the Lakotas. They could rest in the certainty that they would be protected. For the remaining two days of the journey, the chiefs gave no trouble. Reaching Fort Walsh, however, Sitting Bull refused to enter. He had never been in a fort and preferred to camp outside, he said. Again Colonel Macleod prevailed. He turned out all the redcoats to shake the chief's hand and welcome him to the fort, and he stated that there were no Americans inside. Getting Sitting Bull to the fort had been a step-by-step process, but, aided by Macleod, Walsh had succeeded. Sitting Bull told Macleod that he now believed everything the colonel told him, shook his hand, and entered the fort.[7]

Walsh's success in coaxing Sitting Bull into Fort Walsh bore witness to his abilities as a police officer and his influence over Sitting Bull. In America it conferred on him the glow of a public celebrity. The forthcoming meeting with the Americans set off extensive press coverage, in which not only was the feat praised but Walsh himself eulogized in paragraphs of newsprint. He loved it and especially gloried in the label of "Sitting Bull's boss." Some of his subsequent actions reveal that he took that too seriously.

Sitting Bull pitched his lodge apart from the rest of his comrades against the northern wall of the fort. There, with a symbolic red handkerchief tied around his neck, he pursued customary rites of mourning. Two days before the departure from Pinto Horse Butte, his nine-year-old son had died of disease. Grief and ritual therefore hung over the dealings with Walsh and Macleod, making the task of shepherding him to Fort Walsh all the more difficult.[8]

As Macleod had informed Sitting Bull, there were still no Americans in Fort Walsh. They had been delayed. That night, therefore, Sitting Bull called still another council. The chiefs had nothing new to say, but they wanted Walsh advised once again that nothing could persuade them to return to their home country. They knew the Americans would "talk sweet words and make them large promises," but they had been lied to so often they would not believe them this time. Under the protection of the White Mother, they hoped to remain in Canada and raise their children.[9]

Sitting Bull and his chiefs had grudgingly journeyed to Fort Walsh to meet the Americans. They had done this only because Major Walsh had persuaded them. They had arrived to find no Americans, and for four days they anxiously waited. The Canadian officers feared that the Lakotas would use the delay as an excuse to return to Pinto Horse Butte, a course they were in fact considering. The arrival of the commission on the sixteenth, however, ended the worry. The chiefs would meet the Americans the next day.

The council was scheduled for 3:00 p.m. on October 17, leaving the morning to arrange the meeting room. The largest room in the fort, the officers' mess, was commandeered but still left inadequate space for all the participants. At three o'clock commissioners and others took their places. At one table sat Generals Terry and Lawrence, Colonel Corbin, and a stenographer. At a second table sat the two newsmen, Stillson and Diehl. Three interpreters stood nearby, and police officers and various civilians packed themselves against the walls. Scarlet coats and gold braid lent dashes of color. In front of the tables the floor had been spread with buffalo robes to provide seating for the Indians.[10]

With the Sitting Bull Commission in place, Colonel Macleod entered with the first chief, a Miniconjou named Flying Bird, whom he introduced to the commission. Flying Bird shook hands with all at the tables and took his place on the floor. Next came Sitting Bull, accompanied by Major Walsh. Macleod offered his hand and said, "How." Sitting Bull responded quickly, with "How-How," spoken loudly. That set the tone for the meeting. Proceeding to the U.S. commissioners' table, he simply looked at them, mumbled "How," and continued without shaking hands. About thirty chiefs and headmen filed in and took their places on the floor.

Major Walsh seated himself with the commission and Colonel Macleod with the correspondents. Stillson of the *Herald* described Sitting Bull as "silent, stately, and impassive," and displaying a "quiet, ironical smile."

His black hair streamed down along his beardless and swarthy cheeks over clean-cut ears, not burdened with ornaments. His red mourning handkerchief was replaced by a wolfskin cap. His shirt was a black calico specked with white dots. The blanket wrapped negligently around him revealed below its edge a pair of richly beaded moccasins, the only finery he wore.

Not so impassively, Sitting Bull rose from his robes and, pointing at Terry and Lawrence, declared that he wanted them here, pointing at the floor. Terry answered that it was the habit of white people to sit on chairs. Sitting Bull said the chiefs could not see the white men hidden behind the table. Terry and his colleagues grudgingly moved their chairs in front of the table, which put them at a disadvantage without the table to shield them. Sitting Bull was proving adept at handling the Americans.

General Terry had a prepared text and read carefully and slowly, pausing after each sentence for his words to be interpreted. He first made clear that the commissioners had come at the invitation of the Canadian government and that he bore a message from the president of the United States. The message took up many words, but it was essentially that the Lakotas should return to their homes on the same terms as the Indians who had already surrendered. They would be pardoned for any atrocities they had committed. But they had to give up their arms and ammunition before crossing the boundary and then journey to their agencies, where their horses would be taken from them. Both arms and animals would be sold and the proceeds used to buy cattle for them. Meantime they would receive the same rations and clothing as other agency Indians. Concluding, Terry asked the chiefs to take time to ponder the president's words carefully and meet again with the commissioners. They would await the answer.

The official record fails to capture some of the drama of the occasion, but the newsmen were alert. The Indians sat silently, their faces unchanging. On one occasion, however, when Terry said they would be received in a friendly spirit, Sitting Bull smiled. On another, Spotted Eagle winked at Colonel Macleod. After Terry's presentation the Indians sat impassively smoking, smoking, and smoking yet more.

There would be no council to consider the president's words. After the room had filled with smoke Sitting Bull stood and, his words spat out angrily, gave the decision. After his usual description of the wrongs inflicted on his people, he wrathfully asserted: "We did not give you our country. You took it from us. . . . You think me a fool, but you are a greater fool than I am. This is a medicine house. You come to tell us stories, and we do not want to hear them. Don't you say two more words. Go back home where you came from. This country is mine and I intend to stay here." Sitting Bull then turned to Colonel Macleod and Major Walsh and shook their hands. "That is enough; so no more."

The decision of the chiefs, although they had not met in council, could not have been clearer than the tirade Sitting Bull unleashed on the commissioners. Yet four more chiefs made similar abusive speeches. The wife of one of the chiefs also made a speech. Although Terry would not have known it, simply to have a woman in such a venue, and furthermore to have her speak, was a grave insult that the Indians ironically foisted on the U.S. commissioners.

As the Lakotas began to rise, Terry said, "Shall I say to the president that you refuse the offer that he has made to you? Are we to understand from what you have said that you refuse those offers?"

Sitting Bull responded, "I could tell you more, but that is all I have to tell you."

Turning to Colonel Macleod, Terry said, "I think we can have nothing more to say to them, Colonel."

"Well, I suppose you are right," answered the colonel.

"In that case," said Terry, turning to the interpreter, "tell them there is nothing more."

As police surgeon Nevitt wrote, "Sitting Bull in his speech called the Comm'n all kinds of bad names and refused to shake hands with them—pointing this refusal by shaking the hands of all the Police present and even embracing some of them."[11]

In another room Macleod corralled the chiefs to have his own say to them. He emphasized that they should remember that the Queen recognized them as American Indians who had come to the Canadian side of the line to seek protection, that the answer they had just given the commission prevented them ever going south of the boundary with arms in their possession. So long as they behaved themselves, the Queen's government would not drive them out. But they should remember they had to live by the buffalo, and the buffalo would last for only a few more years. They could not expect the Queen's government to feed them when the buffalo vanished.

Macleod then asked for an explanation of what the Americans had done to cause them to leave their country. Of course he already knew, and he should have expected the inevitable response. Sitting Bull gave the same speech he had given so often in the past. Four other chiefs did the same. In reply Macleod made the same speech he and Major Walsh had made before. He addressed a letter to General Terry briefly outlining the words spoken at this meeting. "They unanimously adhered to the answer they had given to the Commission," he concluded.

The Sitting Bull Commission left Fort Walsh the next morning with the Lakota question exactly where it had been when they arrived.

After the meeting with the commission, Charles Diehl of the *Chicago Times* asked Major Walsh if he could interview Sitting Bull. Sitting Bull said no, he would not talk to an American. Walsh finally persuaded him.

With an interpreter, a stenographer, and Walsh, Diehl met Sitting Bull in one of the officers' quarters. Diehl handled it deftly, taking care to be polite and undemanding. Sitting Bull cooperated. What emerged was the first opportunity for Americans to view a human being, alien though he might be, rather than a bloodthirsty savage.[12]

Sitting Bull appeared in the same clothing he wore for the conference, except now he had his red mourning handkerchief hanging loosely around his neck. His long black hair was neatly combed and parted in the middle. Diehl noted that, when speaking, Sitting Bull looked directly into the eyes of the other person and that when he laughed "he does so heartily, that all the stoicism of the savage is gone."

Sitting Bull answered a number of questions about family, his birthplace, his desire for peace, his grievances against the Americans, his intent to stay in Canada, and the subject in which Americans were most interested, the Custer battle. Two responses revealed significant self-estimates.

As for his rise to leadership: "When I was still in my mother's insides, I thought of my people. When my mother bore me, my people were dying with small-pox and other diseases. Then I began to study to help my people. Before I left my mother's insides the God Almighty [Wakantanka] must have told me to think that I could be the judge of all the other Indians, a big man to decide for them."

And so he became. But now he had another belief. He was not a chief or even a head soldier. He was neither, he repeated, as he would in coming months to Major Walsh. "I used to be a chief, but the Americans killed my people and broke up my tribe." Diehl pointed out that today the whites saw all the chiefs looking up to Sitting Bull, as if he were the supreme leader. Why? "It is because I am poor they look up to me." In fact, poverty was a sign of generosity, one of the four cardinal virtues of the Lakotas. But that was not the full explanation, as the Canadian officers later clarified for Diehl. "Sitting Bull is a medicine man," they said. "He is the prophet and seer of his village and has great influence and is virtually their leader."

Sitting Bull's reason for the loss of his chieftainship fails to ring true. He wildly exaggerated American aggressions and their effect. Even if true, they could hardly have deposed a chief of Sitting Bull's mighty stature. Nor did poverty undermine his status. He had always been poor, the result of the generosity ordained by one of the cardinal virtues. The explanation of Canadian officers, combined with dynamic performance before the Sitting Bull Commission, contradicted his self-abdication. But in his own mind, and apparently in the attitudes of the Lakota tribes in Canada, he was no longer the towering chief who said No to the Sitting Bull Commission. That perception would affect the course of his life for the next two years.

The American commissioners had invited Sitting Bull and his people back to their homeland and got Sitting Bull's resounding answer, No. For both the Americans and the Canadians, that firm refusal seemed to settle the question. The Lakotas would remain free in Canada and obey the Queen's laws and rules. For the Canadians, the question now was where to settle them for the long term. Ottawa quickly decided to move Sitting Bull's people far to the north of Wood Mountain, in the Red Deer River district, a tributary of the South Saskatchewan.

Three days after the Sitting Bull Commission adjourned, Colonel Macleod and his officers met with Sitting Bull to tell him about his new home. Sitting Bull responded:

My friend and all the Queen's men whom I so respect: I have heard your talk. I knew you would speak to me in that way. Nobody told me. I just knew it. It is right. I come to you in the first place because I was being hard driven by the Americans. They broke their treaties with my people, and when I rose up and fought, not against them but for our rights as the first people on this part of the earth, they pursued me like a dog, and would have hung me to a tree. They are not just. They drive us into a war, and then seek to punish us for fighting. That is not honest. The Queen would not do that. . . . I heard that she was just and good. Now I know it. . . . I will go to the Red Deer and be at peace. Tell the Queen that.[13]

But Ottawa quickly reversed that decision because it would bring the Lakotas into conflict with the Blackfeet for the shrinking buffalo herds. The Lakotas remained in the vicinity of Wood Mountain, scattered in small camps.[14]

Colonel Macleod had warned Ottawa of the possibility of a clash between Blackfeet and Lakotas. "The Blackfeet are anxious about this invasion of their country," he addressed Prime Minister Mackenzie on May 30, 1877. "They say that before the Canadians arrived they were always able to keep them out, but now they want to be friends."[15]

Sitting Bull wanted to be friends too, but he had no intention of going away. Better yet to try to make friends with the powerful Blackfeet chief Crow Foot. During summer 1877 he succeeded in arranging several meetings with Crow Foot. One in particular went very well. They both smoked the pipe and held it in the four directions as custom dictated, and each declared peace between the two tribes and an end to horse stealing. To exalt his new friend, Sitting Bull named one of his twin sons Crow Foot.[16]

By the end of 1877 both Sitting Bull and the redcoats had become well acquainted. Indeed, all the refugee Lakotas believed they had found friends and protectors in the North-West Mounted Police. For their part, the police had come to admire, and partially trust, the Lakota chiefs, even if they failed to control their young men. At the same time the officers, while dealing in a friendly manner with

the chiefs, heartily agreed with their government that a way had to
be found to persuade the American Indians to return to their homeland, especially since their population was growing.

Beginning in November 1877 Lakotas from south of the boundary came in great numbers, by mid-January 1878 as many as eight
thousand people. Late in November Major Walsh learned that sixty
lodges had arrived in Sitting Bull's camp. He went at once to see who
they were. In council, nine chiefs explained that they had been followers of Crazy Horse. Since his surrender, he had been at the Red
Cloud Agency in Nebraska, but he emerged as a fomenter of trouble with the other Lakota tribes held there. Following his arrest he
had died from a wound inflicted by a soldier's bayonet. The chiefs
quoted Crazy Horse's words as he lay dying:

> I have always wanted to go to the land of the white mother, but
> my father persuaded me to stay here. I shall be dead in a few min-
> utes and will then go to the white mother's country. I want you
> all to follow me; you see the Americans want to kill us. There is
> no peace for you in this country; you can live no longer with the
> Great Father. If you want to live and raise up your families you
> must go with me to the land of the white mother.[17]

From his base at Fort Keogh, Bear Coat Miles had noted the northward movement of Lakotas. They had not gone peaceably. They
had stolen eight or ten horses and twenty-six head of cattle from a
ranch in the Yellowstone Valley. Four ranchers gathered their families and entrenched. Warriors attacked but were held off for four
days. Several Indians were killed, but the citizens escaped unhurt.[18]

With the buffalo herds diminishing noticeably north of the boundary, on December 20, 1877, Major Walsh called Sitting Bull and others
into council. He served notice that henceforth no more buffalo cows
could be killed north of the boundary and prescribed penalties for
violating the order. Uncharacteristically, Sitting Bull replied angrily.
"Who gave you this land and all the buffalo in it? You have not as
much right here as we have, and the Americans put all these mis-

chief making laws in your head. I will cross the line and kill what I like." And he did, despite Walsh's warning that he might have to fight Bear Coat Miles. About eight hundred lodges, sheltering some 2,500 people, established themselves twenty-three miles south of the boundary on Milk River. Sitting Bull surely knew the risk in defying Long Lance, but he got away with it.[19]

Sitting Bull's wrathful outburst is the first recorded suggestion of tension or trouble between him and Walsh. It seems spontaneous and can be explained by the relative roles of the two, which were bound to try the patience of both. In this relationship Sitting Bull stood at a disadvantage. Major Walsh was not really "Sitting Bull's boss"; overseer would describe his role more accurately. But he was responsible for ensuring that Sitting Bull and the Lakotas abided by their promise to remain north of the boundary and obey the White Mother's laws and rules. It is perhaps remarkable that they did not clash more often. Incidents occurred in which Walsh lost his patience, but he rarely lost his temper. This clash between the two is not symptomatic of an enduring hostility, but a warning that such conflicts, given their respective roles, were bound to occur as their relationship persisted.

As Walsh had warned, Bear Coat Miles, in his headquarters at Fort Keogh, quickly learned of Sitting Bull's excursions south of the boundary. He declared that the "whole hostile camp" had come south and joined with Lakotas from the agencies migrating north. He placed their numbers at two thousand fighting men, and he made ready to move against them. General Sherman, however, made it clear that the United States was "not prepared to carry on war against renegade Indians who wander back and forth across the line." "I am not willing," he concluded, "that we should drift into a difficult and expensive war, which may be avoided by leaving time to work out a solution."[20]

Sherman was a wise soldier. He knew his son-in-law to be a highly competent officer who had demonstrated his combat skills both in the Civil War and on the Plains. But he knew him too as prone to let his ambitions overcome his judgment. Sherman was also sensitive to the diplomatic impasse between Canada and the United States taking place in Washington. An offensive thrust toward Canada would likely influence the diplomacy and also prompt Miles, if he thought such pursuit justified, in crossing the boundary into Canada. Sherman also had to take into account Miles's contention that Lakota buffalo hunters in Montana were killing white people and stealing their horses.

Not only buffalo hunters but ambitious young warriors from Wood Mountain. In March 1879 seven Nez Perce and two Lakota warriors killed and wounded settlers on the upper Yellowstone and stole fifty to sixty head of stock. They then returned to Wood Mountain. Miles reported these depredations in a letter to Colonel Macleod at Fort Walsh and sent one of his officers, Lt. John C. F. Tillson, to deliver the dispatch and escort one of the victims to identify his stolen horses. Miles was reprimanded for sending Tillson onto foreign soil, but the mission did establish the reality of depredations committed in Montana by Lakotas living in Canada.[21]

While the Americans talked of war, Major Walsh left for a six-month leave of absence in the East. Early in January 1878 he paused in Ottawa to confer with government officials and collect a contingent of recruits. Superintendent Leif N. F. Crozier took his place overlooking the Lakotas. A stern officer, "Paddy" Crozier viewed the Lakotas less sympathetically than Walsh.

Throughout his six-month absence, passed mostly in his hometown of Brockville, Walsh kept in touch with friends at Wood Mountain, including Lakota leaders, who kept him apprised of the behavior of the Lakotas and especially Sitting Bull. As Walsh advised the minister of the interior in late April 1878, the Indians were acutely aware of what the American newspapers reported from Canada. They constantly alluded to thousands of well-armed warriors gathered along the boundary as if to renew the war with the Americans. Walsh learned from his correspondents of the unrest this caused among the refugees and cautioned against any abrupt movement by the police. The Indians had deduced that at some time in the future Canada and the United States would form an alliance directed at them. The Americans had much money, they reasoned, and were trying to use the White Mother to help them in a war of conquest.

Walsh warned that anything that made the Indians suspect that Canada might form an alliance with the Americans would destroy the influence of the North-West Mounted Police. If the Indians did in fact make a hostile movement across the line, all the Americans should expect from Canada was to notify the U.S. military in Montana and Dakota. He conceded that Canada had some responsibility for Sitting Bull, Spotted Eagle, and others who had been in Canada for a year and had never been agency Indians, but not for those who were even then fleeing from their agencies.[22]

Walsh had learned of Sitting Bull's fears by the time he reached Chicago on his return with the recruits. He had always delighted in talking to newsmen, and in Chicago he had an opportunity. At the Sitting Bull Commission meeting the previous October, he had made friends with Charles Diehl of the *Chicago Times*. On May 20, 1878, Walsh held forth at great length (and to effusive praise from Diehl) on Sitting Bull and other issues involving the resistant Lakotas.[23]

On the central issue of whether Sitting Bull could be induced to return to the United States, Walsh believed that it could be accomplished, but it would take time, as much as five years. Nor could they be persuaded to come all at once but in small bands, the way they had entered Canada. They would eventually come on the same terms General Terry had offered them the previous autumn: surrender their arms and horses to be sold and the returns used to buy cattle for the people. Such a result, he said, would be a blessing for the Lakotas as well as Canada and the United States. Canada did not want these Indians as permanent residents and believed their proper place was on American reservations. (In his prediction, Walsh proved remarkably prescient.) Walsh did not believe there was any prospect of a hostile move by Sitting Bull. From all the reports he had received, peace still prevailed.

But, according to Walsh, Sitting Bull no longer reigned as head chief, a condition he had heard Sitting Bull explain to newsman Charles Diehl in the interview at the conclusion of the Terry meeting:

> He has continued to lose caste among the savages since the interview with the Americans, and to-day he has no following. From a letter I received a few days ago, I am told that all the Uncapapa Indians have joined the village of Spotted Eagle, and that that warrior is now the head man among the hostiles. Sitting Bull is still located a little south of the Cypress Hills, and has with him only five lodges, which are mainly made up of his own family and relatives. Sitting Bull has consequently lost all his former greatness.

Further evidence for his decline in prestige rests almost entirely on Sitting Bull's taking up residence with only a few Hunkpapas or Sans Arcs periodically over the next two years. The explanation remained locked in Sitting Bull's mind and may have led to some of his bolder actions in subsequent months,

Why, or even if, this was true, it did not apply to his immediate following, as demonstrated by an incident that occurred in summer 1878. According to Old Bull, Sitting Bull's brother-in-law Gray Eagle attended a horse-racing contest with a nearby camp of Slotas, Red River mixed-bloods. Three comrades went with him: White Cow Walking, White Bird, and Good Crow. One of the Slotas had an exceptionally fine horse. Gray Eagle and his three companions stole that horse and a hundred more, rode south, and swung back to Wood Mountain. They hid the horses behind a ridge and then entered Sitting Bull's camp. The theft was already known, and nephew One Bull summoned the camp akicitas. They went to Sitting Bull's lodge and confronted Gray Eagle. Sitting Bull ordered Gray Eagle to retrieve the horses and for the akicitas to fire over his head as he went. They did, inflicting public humiliation. When Gray Eagle returned to submit to further punishment, his wife, Sitting Bull's sister, began to cry. Sitting Bull yielded on Gray Eagle but not the other three. They were stripped naked and forced to the ground. Their ankles were tied down with forked sticks and their wrists bound to the sticks. Swarms of mosquitos intensified the agony of a blazing sun beating down each day. With two guards, the three remained in this position for a week. Their release was followed by a big feast. "This was a good lesson for the whole tribe," recalled Old Bull, "and no more laws were broken."

Gray Eagle and Good Eagle searched for all the stolen horses but could not find them all. The Hunkpapa chiefs made up the deficit from their own herds, and the entire number were returned to the Slotas.[24]

Despite renegade warriors crossing the border into the United States, stealing horses and inflicting depredations on whites; despite a number of spirited disagreements with his new white friends; and despite his loss of stature among his people, Sitting Bull and the resistance continued and flourished.

4

Fall and Rise

Contrasting with the previous winter, winter 1878–79 was severe, with biting cold and deep snow. Both Indians and police had great difficulty in plowing their way through the snow, but both persisted. Also, in contrast, the buffalo grew scarcer, bringing hunger and unrest to the Lakotas, who were now refugees struggling to survive. Blackfeet and other Canadian tribes competed for the buffalo and resented the intruders. The Lakota camps were scattered from Wood Mountain to the boundary, and hunters slipped across to assail the more numerous herds south of the U.S. line.

With the coming of summer the snows melted, and the scattered bands welcomed Major Walsh back from his long leave. With a squad of troopers, Walsh went among the Lakotas living in the vicinity of Wood Mountain. He discovered Sitting Bull still struggling with the consequences of his self-proclaimed loss of the head chieftainship. Once he had been head chief of the Hunkpapa tribe, then as recently as ten years ago anointed head chief of all the Lakota tribes. He had led them, and they had followed him. Crossing the "medicine line" into Canada had not diminished his power. He was still the supreme leader when he entered the gates of Fort Walsh on October 12, 1877. And at no time had he asserted his dominance as emphatically as in facing down General Terry. Yet only a day after humiliating the general, he declared that he was not a chief. He behaved as if he was not a chief, and the Lakotas seemed no longer to look up to him as a chief.

The surviving documents for 1878–79, mainly those penned by Major Walsh, take no note of Sitting Bull's frame of mind. If he and his people did not embrace the decline he professed, why did he abandon his own Hunkpapa tribe and live for more than a year with the Sans Arcs? The Hunkpapas camped twenty miles west of Wood Mountain Post, and the Sans Arcs twenty miles to the south, on White Mud Creek four miles north of the Oglalas and twelve miles north of the international boundary. When the Sans Arcs decided to move north to Wood Mountain for the winter, however, Sitting Bull and five lodges remained behind. They did not immediately join the nearby Hunkpapas but camped two miles to the west. Once he crossed the line and stayed for seven days, acquiring meat for his family.

Sitting Bull then moved back to the Hunkpapas west of Wood Mountain Post. There he was exposed to Major Walsh's constant effort to persuade him and the other Lakotas to go back to their homeland. Sitting Bull's mind remained clear on that point. He would never go back.

This did not represent the opinion of all leaders in his and other Lakota camps. As the buffalo thinned and the people went hungry, others openly proclaimed their wish to seek the comforts of their agencies. To accomplish this, they still encountered the rule that no one left without the permission of the village council, a rarity given the attitude of Sitting Bull. To defy this requirement risked "soldiering" by One Bull's police, the akicita.

In the first week of October 1878 Sitting Bull and his brother came to Wood Mountain Post to talk with Long Lance. For two days they talked, Walsh striving to convince Sitting Bull of the wisdom of returning to his homeland. Again he failed. Sitting Bull was determined never to return to the United States, alleging a fear of assassination "from roughs about the agencies." This of course was not the reason. He had vowed to live in Canada, and he would honor that vow.[1]

For the second time, One Bull acutely embarrassed Sitting Bull. That his trusted and beloved nephew should bring dishonor on his uncle belied his generally upstanding character. One Bull paid secret court to a Miniconjou maiden who was betrothed to a Miniconjou warrior and impregnated her. As the time arrived when she could no longer conceal her pregnancy, she tied herself to a high tree limb jutting over a high bank. She jumped and the shock aborted the fetus. The ordeal prostrated her in her lodge. Learning of her infidelity, her paramour rushed into her lodge and shot and killed her. So angry was he that he forgot to ask her who the guilty party was, but the truth eventually emerged. A party of Miniconjous set forth for Sitting Bull's camp, intent on vengeance. Once again, however, the diplomacy of Sitting Bull rescued his nephew.[2]

Early in November runners brought word to Sitting Bull of more Lakotas, and even Cheyenne allies, approaching from below the boundary to seek refuge with their kinsmen in Canada. Walsh soon appeared at Sitting Bull's lodge. He had received the same word, and he feared that Lakotas from north of the boundary would hasten south to aid them. In council, with other chiefs seated with him, Sitting Bull promised Walsh to do nothing to help the fugitives and to send word to the Oglalas of his determination. But he and some of his people, he declared, intended to move close to the boundary to observe events. He would not go south of the boundary, but if U.S. troops crossed into Canada he and his people would fight.[3]

Sitting Bull awoke on November 4 to discover Walsh and a squad of constables camped nearby. He sent the major a message proposing that the next day the two ride together to the Oglala camp and persuade them not to interfere. Walsh accepted. This would provide an opportunity for him to talk with Sitting Bull in less formal circumstances than usual.

During the ride, Walsh asked Sitting Bull's opinion about whether the agency Indians coming from the south could elude American troops and succeed in reaching the boundary and, if they did, whether the Hunkpapa and Oglala warriors were likely to go to their aid. Walsh also asked a pertinent question: if these people did get across the boundary, how did they propose to feed themselves?

Sitting Bull had ready answers, which he expounded at length. Yes, the agency Indians could easily reach Canada. They did not fear the soldiers. To the Lakotas, all the troops on the Missouri and

Yellowstone Rivers appeared as only one man; they might look like many soldiers, but they had the strength of only one. The American was born with a gun in his hand but did not know how to use it. The Lakotas with their stone coup sticks would fight and defeat them, even with their guns.

As for how the newcomers would feed themselves in Canada, that was simple. The Great Spirit (Wakantanka) had provided for these people until now. If they reached Canada, the Great Spirit would still look after them.

Walsh and Sitting Bull discovered the Oglala camp on the White Mud Creek, located only half a mile north of the boundary and on the road their friends were expected to use. The two agreed that was too close. It might entice the young men to cross and fight U.S. troops. Walsh asked Sitting Bull to ride into the camp and tell Chief Big Road and the men in the war lodge that they would please Long Lance very much if they would move back from the boundary. Two hours later, all four hundred Oglala lodges had packed and were moving north. They stopped for the night ten miles from the line, then proceeded to join Sitting Bull's main Hunkpapa village northwest of Wood Mountain Post.

While the Oglala camp moved out, the chiefs with a multitude of warriors convened a council on a nearby hilltop. They invited Walsh to sit with them. The chiefs talked of an issue that had tormented them for a long time: what if American troops crossed the line? In earlier councils Walsh and his colleagues had dealt with this matter, but it continued to disturb the Indians. The Long Knives would not cross, asserted Walsh, unless they were pursuing Lakotas from Canada who had crossed to the south and committed depredations. In that event the White Mother might allow the troops to cross. What would Walsh do if the Americans crossed and fired on the Lakotas? He would confront the American commander and place him under arrest. A skeptical Sitting Bull concluded the council:

> The Americans are like snakes, he will not listen to you, and you have but few men and cannot force him. I am now going to my

camp to look after my young men to see that they do not cross the line. If the American crosses the line and does not listen to you, send me word and every young man in camp will mount his horse and come to your assistance.[4]

If any refugees crossed the line, they were small enough in number to escape notice. The alarm of the police and Indians turned out to have been unwarranted. But the exercise had the positive effect of bringing Sitting Bull and Walsh closer together. The conversation on the ride from the Hunkpapa camp to the Oglala camp helped bond the two and heighten the trust and perhaps even friendship.

That bond was soon to be tested. In mid-December 1878 the refugee Nez Perce chief White Bird staged a feast to which he invited Sitting Bull and some Lakota headmen. He announced that in September some Nez Perces had been in the camps of Crow Indians south of the boundary, and the Crows had raised the possibility of an alliance with both Lakotas and Nez Perces. The Crows feared that the Americans verged on taking their guns and horses. It seemed as if Americans and Canadians were friends and that, if they could not force the Lakotas and Nez Perces to return to their homes, the Canadians would open the boundary to U.S. troops. At White Bird's feast the chiefs and headmen decided to form a delegation to carry tobacco to the Crows and invite them to join the Nez Perces and Lakotas in Canada. Sitting Bull concurred in this decision.[5]

Curiously, after their first overtures to White Bird the Crows angrily refused the tobacco. For a century or more they had been mortal enemies of the Lakotas. So affronted were they that their answer to the tobacco was a sudden raid on the Lakotas' horse herd that carried away one hundred horses.

Infuriated by the costly betrayal, Sitting Bull summoned his chiefs and warriors to his lodge to plan revenge. He had been moving his dwelling back and forth across the border, and when the council took place on January 23, 1879, he was south of the border. Even so, among the participants was Major Walsh, who had braved deep snow to sit with the Lakota leaders.

The war council turned into an argument between Sitting Bull and Walsh. The White Mother had promised protection, Sitting Bull reminded Walsh, and now she had let the Crows steal his horses. What would she do about it? Walsh countered with his own reproach. "I believe you and the Nez Perces are to blame for this raid. If you had not tried to plant sedition in the Crow tribe . . . the Crows would never have sent their young men into the White Mother's country to steal horses from the Lakotas."

He did indeed send messengers to the Crows, Sitting Bull admitted defiantly. If the Crows joined him, he believed he would be strong enough to fight the Americans if they attacked. Now that he had been attacked, he would fight back. "I wish you to tell the White Mother that I will do to the Americans [Crows?] as they have done to me. It is not my wish to go to war, but I must. I never told you I was a chief; today I tell you I am one." This was a surprising statement, suggesting that Sitting Bull had regained his old stature.

Probably aware that he was on the American side of the line, Walsh closed the council with the admonition that Sitting Bull should consider carefully what he planned. If carried out it would place him and his people in great jeopardy.[6]

Sitting Bull did reconsider, or at least resolved to make amends to Major Walsh for his brash words. On March 23, 1879, he appeared at Wood Mountain Post. Most of the chiefs of the Hunkpapas and Miniconjous accompanied him. They seated themselves in Long Lance's quarters. Sitting Bull explained that he had not meant to make war but only to defend himself. "What I wish to say to the White Mother is that I have but one heart and it is the same today as when I first shook your hand." He would never again talk to an American general or shake hands with an American. He would never go back to his homeland. And he would never farm, as the Americans wanted him to do. "I will remain what I am until I die. I am a hunter, and when there are no buffalo or other game I will send my children to hunt and live on prairie mice for where an Indian is shut up in one place his body becomes weak."

"I am looking to the north for my life," he concluded. Any of his people who wished to return south could do so. Those who did not could stay and live with him. As Walsh quickly noted, this represented a major concession. Previously Sitting Bull had opposed anyone leaving, even to the point of using akicita to prevent them. Now, having proclaimed that he was indeed a chief, he would let them go. This momentous concession forecast the fatal erosion of his following.[7]

Another reality promised trouble. Very few buffalo grazed north of the boundary, and in the snow-drifted country the Lakota horses were too weak to make many rides to the south, where the buffalo were more plentiful. At the time of this meeting, his people were scattered in hunting camps in the Milk River country of Montana, fair game for Bear Coat Miles and his soldiers. The White Mother could not protect them there. "All I am looking for is something for my children to eat. But I will not remain south of the line one day more than I can help."[8]

He stayed not only one day longer but many days longer. Throughout winter 1878–79 he bounced back and forth across the border but kept north of it enough to meet with Walsh. Both knew that he had violated the terms on which he and his people were allowed to settle in Canada. Sitting Bull had been told unequivocally that he must remain north of the border or lose the protection of the White Mother. If he crossed he could not return. But he had crossed and he had returned, and Long Lance had indulged him. The Lakotas were hungry, and they would go to where the meat was. If the young men chose to raid white ranches and steal their horses, that was what young men did.

In fact, both Sitting Bull and Walsh were in an untenable position. Ottawa demanded that the Lakotas go back to their agencies, and Walsh had the mission of persuading or forcing them to do that. Sitting Bull believed that returning would cost him his life or at best force him to live an unendurable life. Walsh understood, as Ottawa seemed not to, that the Lakotas had to eat, and that meant going to where the meat was. So for both the dilemma persisted.

Sitting Bull had his rationale, as he explained to *Chicago Tribune* correspondent Stanley Huntley in mid-June 1879. Sitting Bull and other prominent chiefs, including Big Road, were camped on Milk River, forty-five miles south of the boundary. Huntley's long article was phrased in florid language, but Sitting Bull's thinking emerged clearly.

If Sitting Bull remained south of the border and the Long Knives attacked him, what would he do? asked Huntley. "You cannot go back to the white mother. Where can you go?"

Two years ago [the chief explained] we went on the white mother's lands; there many children have been born; are they not the children of the white mother? Will she drive her children from the country where they were born? No; she will let them stay there. Will she separate them from their fathers and mothers? No; she will protect her children born on her soil, and she will protect the fathers and mothers of these children.'

Sitting Bull's belief was not irrational. It made sense to him and perhaps even to Major Walsh. But it neglected two realities: shrinking buffalo herds and the firm policy of Ottawa. Both would combine to undermine this rationale.

The flaw in the reasoning was Bear Coat Miles. Since 1876 Sitting Bull had been his special target, as also the prime villain to the American public. If Miles had his way, he would cross the boundary and root out the Lakotas, as indeed they constantly feared. Short of that, he wanted to launch a campaign north of the Missouri in the Milk River country, where a variable number of Lakotas could usually be found hunting buffalo. If he had had the independent command he kept pressing General Sherman for, he would have undertaken such a move. But his superiors kept him restrained.

"You must watch and see that Genl Miles does not precipitate trouble near our Northern border," General Sherman advised General Sheridan.

Genl Miles is too apt to mistake the dictates of his personal ambition for wisdom, and I am very sorry that he is not just and fair
to his comrades and superiors. He will absorb all power to himself and ignore his immediate commanders if not supervised and
checked. I am thus frank with you lest you think I am disposed
to encourage him in his restless action, which he sometimes mis-
takes for a contrast to other officers disposed to await orders &
instructions. I have done him hundreds of favors but because I
withhold one he forgets all else.[10]

The general of the army knew Miles all too well. For almost a
decade he had bombarded his wife's uncle with appeals for special
preferment, which Sherman met with refusals borne of his distaste
for nepotism. Indeed, Sherman wrote this letter the day after a colli-
sion between Miles and Sitting Bull. Bear Coat was even then moving
north toward the boundary.

The president, the secretary of war, Generals Sherman and Sheridan, and Miles's commander General Terry all opposed an offensive
movement against Sitting Bull. The stalemated diplomatic negotiations in Washington, hanging on the issue of whether the United
States or Canada should have responsibility for Sitting Bull, roiled
relations between the two countries as well as the United Kingdom,
which handled the dominion's foreign affairs. Fear of an expensive
Indian war haunted the top officials.

As became increasingly apparent, however, throughout the opening months of 1879 Sitting Bull's people ranged Montana's Milk River
country hunting buffalo, angering the Yanktonais, who regarded
these buffalo as theirs, and occasionally depredating as far south as
the Yellowstone. The Indian agent at Fort Peck vigorously protested
the turmoil sweeping his jurisdiction.[11]

Queried about the agent's outcry, General Terry advised that the
only way to stop Lakota incursions across the border was to send
a strong column against them, but he had not done so because of
administration policy. Despite the risk, however, he gained approval.
On June 5, 1879, Terry authorized Miles to undertake this mission,

"to force the Lakotas back rather by a show of force than by actual conflict." Whatever the strictures, Miles had been cut loose, and, as Terry surely knew from experience, he would act as he wanted, which indeed included "actual conflict."[12]

In March 1879 Sitting Bull had relaxed his ban on people moving south to surrender, and by May about one hundred lodges were packing to leave. But runners brought word that Bear Coat was assembling a large force of soldiers to take the field against Sitting Bull. As the press reported, "The Sioux chiefs say they don't want to fight particularly, but their children cry for meat and they must have it. They will fight any force that gets between them and the buffalo."[13] Sitting Bull and the main village lay ten miles north of the boundary while a large body of hunters camped on Milk River in Montana. Sitting Bull crossed to join them.[14] The camp lay opposite the mouth of Beaver Creek, a southern tributary of the Milk. On July 13 Sitting Bull was in this camp. Several hundred hunters had brought down enough buffalo to meet immediate needs. They collected the carcasses for the women to butcher. Most of the men left to return across the boundary. Sitting Bull was among those who remained with the women to help pack the meat.

Suddenly they spotted horsemen riding toward them down the slope across the river. The men prepared for a fight. But the approaching riders carried rifles with red bandanas tied to them, which seemed to signify a desire for a parley. The Lakotas withheld their fire until it became apparent that these men were enemies, not friends, and then drew up in line for a fight. The aggressors were Crow and other Indians whose red bandanas identified them as scouts for the soldiers. They too formed a line of battle.

One of the Indian scouts advanced in front of his lines bearing a white flag. He was Magpie, a renowned Crow, a powerful warrior, and the son of an influential chief. For a long time he had boasted to American officers that if he could make direct contact with Sitting Bull, they would no longer be troubled by him. Under a white flag Magpie rode forward and faced the Lakota line. A Lakota warrior rode out to meet Magpie, who asked if Sitting Bull was among this group. Informed that he was, Magpie declared that he wanted to meet him in personal combat.

Sitting Bull accepted the challenge. He mounted, hoisted his rifle into firing position, and trotted in front of the Lakota lines to face Magpie. Magpie did the same and closed on Sitting Bull. Magpie raised his rifle, aimed at his opponent, and pulled the trigger. His weapon misfired. Sitting Bull aimed, fired, and knocked Magpie from his horse, dead. Sitting Bull calmly dismounted, scalped his challenger, remounted and rode away, leading Magpie's horse, which was now his.

For his people, such a feat ratified Sitting Bull's stature as a great leader.[15]

Troops and their Indian allies advanced on the Lakotas, who fell back in disorder. But their pursuers were merely the advance guard of the main column and numbered less than one hundred. When the retreating warriors caught up with the rest of the hunters, the combined body numbered four hundred. These all turned to confront the soldiers and scouts and completely surrounded them. Before they could do much damage, however, Miles, having been alerted by courier, led the main command onto the field. He deployed his artillery, which lobbed explosive rounds into the Lakotas. They turned quickly and hastened north.

Miles followed, but his ponderous command could not travel as fast as the Lakotas. Moreover, the weather made both traveling and fighting difficult. As the *Chicago Times* correspondent complained, "The weather is damnable. It rains most of the time. The sun is very hot, and the roads are horrible."[16] For both Indian and soldier, field work was miserable.

When Miles reached the boundary, he found that the Lakotas had already crossed.[17]

The American force camped three-fourths of a mile south of the boundary, and there on July 24 Major Walsh conferred with Miles. Walsh told Miles that he had orders to notify him of any hostile acts by the Lakotas, but he was uncertain if hunting to avert starvation counted as a hostile act. The Lakotas had crossed to Milk River only because literally they possessed no food. Had they not encountered the American soldiers, they would have returned peacefully to the Canadian side. In fact, Canadian authorities regarded crossing for food a necessity, not as an act of hostile intent. Starving Indians should not be held responsible for crossing the boundary.[18]

That made no difference, responded Miles. His orders were to prevent the Indians from crossing into American territory. The Milk River country was a Yanktonai Indian reservation. The buffalo ranging it belonged to the Yanktonais, not the Lakotas. He had reports, moreover, that these hunters stole stock from white ranchers and killed white settlers. He wanted the culprits seized. If the Lakotas wished to come south for any purpose, they had to surrender their horses and guns and settle at an agency. Miles asked Walsh to meet with the Lakotas in Canada and urge them to adopt this course, then return with their answer. Two years' experience had taught Walsh what the answer would be, but he agreed.[19]

Chicago Times correspondent John F. Finerty, who had accompanied Miles from Fort Keogh, sat watching this exchange. He badly wanted to interview Sitting Bull, so he rode with Walsh and his escort back to Wood Mountain Post, then on to the Hunkpapa village. The two with their escort rode into the village on July 30. They arrived in the midst of a raucous scalp dance staged by Chief Big Road. All the other chiefs and their people, including Sitting Bull, were present. Walsh called an immediate council to convey what Bear Coat had said.

When all had settled, Walsh opened the council:

I have come from the camp of the white chief Bear's Robe. He says none of you must go south of the line which has been shown you, and which will be your protection as long as you behave yourselves. The white mother cannot protect you if you violate her laws. Your hunting parties must not cross the boundary in search of buffalo or other game. Wait until they come here. They are heading this way now. I saw droves of them near the line as I came in. Your men can chase them after they come into the white mother's country. . . .

One thing is certain—you cannot be permitted to violate the laws.
I am willing to do all I can to aid you, within the law.

At this point a warrior rode into the circle and said something to the
Hunkpapas. The interpreter related that two young men had crossed
the boundary pursuing buffalo. Miles's Cheyenne scouts had killed
one and wounded the other. Walsh resumed:

Your young men will not hear what I say, and, consequently, they
must suffer the consequences. If they had kept here, as I asked
them, nothing fatal would have occurred to them. So long as you
remain deaf to my counsel, so long there will be death at your
doors and mourning in your tepees.[20]

Buffalo were indeed coming, which offered the prospect of food
and therefore of the promised end to cross-border incursions. Canadian officers, however, well knew that the buffalo were disappearing
and that soon both refugee American Indians and native Canadians
would face vanishing herds. Canada could feed the Canadians as
the Americans did their own tribes, but the Canadian government
regarded the refugee Lakotas as the responsibility of the United
States, which in turn viewed them as Canada's responsibility. The
diplomatic stalemate festered in Washington.

The Lakota chiefs could more readily pledge not to cross the boundary for any purpose than agree to give up. As Walsh informed his
superiors, "Such is their determination not to surrender to the United
States authorities that I think they will actually die of starvation
before they will return."[21]

As promised, Walsh was back in Miles's camp with the Lakota
answer on July 28. The prominent chief Long Dog accompanied
him. Their report was so complete and persuasive that even a bel-
ligerent officer like Miles was convinced. He reported: "They say the
entire hostile camp is moving north and spreading out near some
lakes about eighty miles north of the boundary. They give assurances that the hostile Indians—Hunkpapa, Miniconjous, Oglalas,

Sans Arcs, and a few other tribes, estimated at 5,000 to 8,000—have decided to remain on Canadian soil and that they will make no hostile movement to this side. They will stop all raiding parties, return all stolen property brought to their camp, and will not hunt buffalo or disturb the game on this reservation unless permitted under the surveillance of U.S. officials. In brief, they are determined to remain in that territory, under the Canadian authorities." These assurances by Long Dog and the Canadian officer, Miles concluded, made it safe to recommend withdrawing his command—uncharacteristically pacific for that warrior.[22]

The Lakota chiefs seemed sincere in their pledge to remain north of the boundary. As long as the buffalo grazed in their vicinity and the redcoats quit nagging them to return to their homeland, they had ample incentive.

Despite the seemingly favorable outcome of Walsh's mission, he had no sooner returned to Wood Mountain Post than, on July 31, three days after their conference, he telegraphed Miles seeking permission for the Lakotas in Canada to cross the boundary to hunt buffalo for food. Walsh believed they had no hostile intent. If permission were granted, the Indians would cross, hunt, and return at once without committing depredations. This request, he added, was made to prevent starvation and great suffering. Walsh knew the Americans would not accept such a measure, so his missive must have been simply for the record.

Miles's endorsement on Major Walsh's missive to General Terry did not abruptly rule out consent, as would ordinarily be his custom, but he killed it anyway. If this proposal were approved, as an act of charity, it could only be carried out under military surveillance and only as long as it took the Lakotas in Canada to become a pastoral or agricultural people.[23]

As the astute newsman John Finerty observed, "The English now have an elephant on their hands which they will find it hard to get rid of." Their best means in 1879, he wrote, appeared to lie in "Maj. Walsh, who has a genuine sympathy for the Lakotas, and also, at present, wields more influence with them than any white man now living."

1. Sitting Bull, photographed after he had surrendered and settled at Standing Rock Reservation. Montana Historical Society Research Center Archives.

2. Maj. James Morrow Walsh, North-West Mounted Police, Sitting Bull's overseer in Canada for three years. Glenbow Museum, Calgary, Alberta.

3. Fort Walsh, Saskatchewan, in 1878. Glenbow Museum, Calgary, Alberta.

4. NWMP officers at Fort Walsh, 1879. Glenbow Museum, Calgary, Alberta.

5. One Bull, Sitting Bull's nephew and constant companion. State Historical Society of North Dakota A-4515.

6. Gall, powerful chief in Sitting Bull's camp. State Historical Society of North Dakota, col. 22H90.

7. Crow King, Hunkpapa war chief and Sitting Bull's head soldier, photographed in an army major's uniform. State Historical Society of North Dakota, C-486.

8. Col. Nelson A. Miles, "Bear Coat" to the Lakotas, guarded the international border to clash with any Lakotas who crossed from Canada back into the United States. Montana Historical Society.

9. Sitting Bull and Maj. Acheson Irvine confer in council held June 2,
1877. Drawing by Police Surgeon William Nevitt. Glenbow Museum,
Calgary, Alberta.

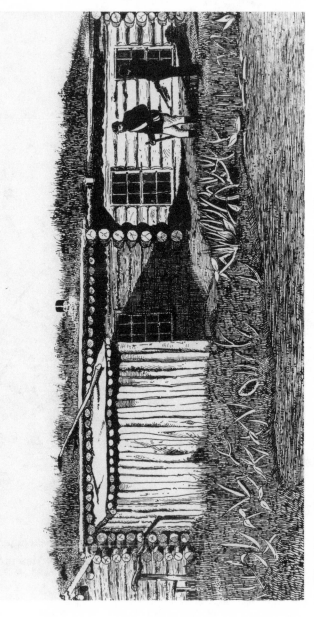

10. Wood Mountain Post, Saskatchewan, headquarters of Major Walsh while dealing with Sitting Bull, 1877–80. Glenbow Museum, Calgary, Alberta.

11. Acheson G. Irvine, Commissioner of the North-West Mounted Police, 1880–86. Library and Archives Canada / Vernon Lachance Collection, C-030725.

12. Sketch of Sitting Bull Council at Fort Walsh, October 13, 1877. Engraving from *New York Graphic*. Glenbow Museum, Calgary, Alberta.

SITTING BULL.

13. Sitting Bull as sketched by journalist Jerome Stillson at Sitting Bull Commission in October 1877. It was the first likeness to appear in public print. *New York Herald*, December 8, 1877. Glenbow Museum, Calgary, Alberta.

14. Supt. Leif N. F. Crozier, North-West Mounted Police, 1880. He succeeded Major Walsh in charge of Sitting Bull and Wood Mountain Post. Glenbow Museum, Calgary, Alberta.

15. Jean Louis Legaré, trader at Wood Mountain and then Willow Bunch, coaxed Sitting Bull to surrender. R-A1875, Jean Louis Legaré, courtesy of the Provincial Archives of Saskatchewan.

16. Maj. David H. Brotherton, U.S. Army Commander of Fort Buford. Brotherton received Sitting Bull's surrender on July 20, 1881. Paul L. Hedren Collection.

17. Capt. Walter Clifford, U.S. Army, met and accompanied Sitting Bull to surrender at Fort Buford. Paul Hedren Collection.

18. Procession of Sitting Bull and followers arriving at Fort Buford to surrender, July 19, 1881. Sketch in *Harper's Weekly*. State Historical Society of North Dakota, B-1636.

5

Creeping Uncertainty

As 1879 neared its end, Sitting Bull had given no sign that he had changed his mind about his future. He wished to remain free in Canada. To all who urged him to return to his homeland, he had responded with the emphatic NO that he had hurled at General Terry. Major Walsh prodded him incessantly, seemingly to no avail. Sitting Bull had lifted the ban on others of his tribe and consented to their return if they wanted. For his part, however, he was "looking to the north for my life."

Winter 1879–80 was as harsh as the previous one, with deep snow confining the Lakotas to their lodges except when hunger forced a quick hunt. But the buffalo were hard to find because autumn prairie fires had swept the grasslands from the Rocky Mountains to Wood Mountain, and animals had trouble finding sustenance under deep snow. Sitting Bull and his followers camped in small groups on Frenchmen's Creek and Milk River.

With the coming of spring 1880, the persuasions of Major Walsh and the specter of starvation swayed large numbers of Lakotas. In March the first movement south took place, thirty lodges. In the next four months, wrote Walsh, "another party left, and then another, . . until the great camp of 1,000 lodges of 1879 was reduced to about 50 lodges of Sitting Bull's own relatives." Walsh said Sitting Bull wanted to go with them but feared the U.S. government would treat him worse than his people. That these thoughts were indeed running through his mind is indicated by the feelers he put out to friends at the agencies: how would he be received? Would he be punished?

Walsh had talked a lot with him about the Little Bighorn and tried to assure him that the Americans would not punish him for that.[1]

On May 19, 1880, Sitting Bull told Walsh that he intended to remain in Canada but declared that he was prepared to shake hands with the Americans and end all feeling of hostility. "These are words never spoken and sentiments never felt by me before. Today I show you my heart. You can make known my feelings."[2]

Indeed, he had never spoken these words before. What did they mean? He intended to live in Canada, but shaking hands with the Americans implied surrender, with all of its conditions. In light of what was taking place at that very time, his words either meant confusion or scheming. Only four days later, on May 23, his nephew One Bull carried out a dangerous mission on behalf of his uncle.

Not solely in Canada but for years before that, One Bull had been his uncle's trusted advisor and companion, and the man to carry out any mission prescribed by Sitting Bull. Tall, muscular, and handsome, One Bull served as chief of Sitting Bull's akicita, which made him a person of consequence in the village.

He was also brave; only a very brave Lakota could enter Fort Buford, Dakota, where Indian prisoners were kept, and present himself to the commanding officer, Lt. Col. Daniel Huston.

Huston conducted the interview, although he got the name wrong, calling him Young Eagle. One Bull used blunt language: "We don't want to fight any longer, the people are all coming in. During all this time we have never struck the first blow, we have always been attacked." Then he delivered a message from Sitting Bull:

My father was a chief, but they cast me out of their camp and left me in the prairie. I have been driven a long way, beyond my country, to the last point I can be driven to, and I want to know who is doing it (meaning what is it all for), and I want to know what you will do with us if we will surrender. If it is good, I will come. If not, I won't. I will wait until the young man gets back. He represents my people.

That was the essence of the message. But he diminished its power by adding that he wanted a trading post built just for him. He was driven out of his country by the white man, and now he wanted to be paid for the country he had lost.

Colonel Huston replied that a message had just been received from the Great Father's war chief. It was sent to all the forts on the Missouri River. It said that Sitting Bull and his people had to come in and surrender their ponies and arms. These were the same terms that had always been offered, and none other would be. If Sitting Bull would come in, he would be given plenty to eat. He would be sent to one of the agencies or a new one. That was Washington's talk, Huston said. Huston's talk was that Sitting Bull should come in now and surrender; he and his people had to do it sometime.[3]

One Bull's report to his uncle of Colonel Huston's reply may have put both in such a bad frame of mind that it contributed to, if not caused, the crisis that occurred only a few days after One Bull's return from Fort Buford.

Among the Wood Mountain traders, the Lakotas had no better friend than Jean Louis Legaré. The Wood Mountain trader treated the Lakotas fairly, even generously, when they brought their robes in for trade. On June 2, 1880, One Bull foolishly stole one of Legaré's horses.

In 1880 Jean Louis was serving as justice of the peace. He appointed two men as special constables and sent them to bring the culprit to face the magistrate. They returned to report that the Indian refused to come. Jean Louis then asked Major Walsh to make the arrest. Walsh turned the task over to his sergeant major, who dispatched a corporal, a constable, and an interpreter to enter the Hunkpapa village, half a mile distant, and bring One Bull to the post. Sitting Bull intervened to advise his nephew not to go because, he predicted, the police would tie him up. Instead Sitting Bull would go to the post and settle the issue with Major Walsh. If that failed, he said, One Bull must make his escape from the camp.

The corporal had not been ordered to use force and sent to the post for further instructions. Walsh sent his sergeant major and four men to aid the corporal in making the arrest and ordered him not to return without One Bull. Observing these redcoats approaching, One Bull decided to go with the corporal to the post as instructed.

At the post, Walsh told Legaré's special constable to mount his horse and ride to the trading post to summon Jean Louis. At this moment Sitting Bull rode up and seized the horse's reins. Frightened, the constable jumped off. Walsh ordered the sergeant major to return the horse to the constable. When he had mounted, One Bull ran over and seized the reins of the horse. Walsh pushed him aside and told Sitting Bull that if he touched the horse again there would be bloodshed, and the onus would lie on him. The major later conceded that he had every intention of shooting Sitting Bull if he disobeyed.

At the entrance to the post, a swelling crowd of Hunkpapa men had gathered to watch the drama. Tensions mounted rapidly, both among the onlookers, now numbering about one hundred, and in front of the Wood Mountain Post. Redcoats dragged One Bull to the gate through which to thrust him into the fort. Women ran from the Hunkpapa village bearing rifles and belts of cartridges to give to their men, who were trying to rescue One Bull. Sitting Bull yelled for One Bull to resist.

The warriors shouted and raised their rifles as, even after One Bull was securely inside, they converged on the gates. Walsh formed his available force of redcoats, twelve men, in a line facing the approaching horde, Enfield carbines at the ready. Above all the clamor, Walsh roared that he was the chief here and they had one minute to disperse before his men opened fire. They dispersed.

Summoned by Walsh, Justice of the Peace Legaré came to the post, held court, and freed One Bull.

Throughout their relationship, neither Sitting Bull nor Walsh had experienced a crisis of this magnitude. In a council convened that night in the Hunkpapa village, Sitting Bull declared that he had just had the narrowest escape of his life, that he was sure that had he touched the horse again, he would have been killed. But, he said, "his heart was bad, as he had been told he was a rascal, and driven away from the post like a dog." The next morning he packed to leave. He told the post interpreter that he had lost his chance of ever getting anything on this side of the line, so would try to make arrangements to go to a U.S. agency.

At the council the night before, Sitting Bull's version of the clash did not go uncontested. Another chief rose to point out that if they wanted to live in this country, they had to obey the White Mother's laws. Major Walsh, he said, was like their own Crazy Horse, not afraid to die in making them do what he told them. That night a delegation of Oglalas under Stone Dog came to tell Walsh that they had come to this country to obey the laws, and in any trouble like today they would help the police and if necessary fight on their side. The next day Big Road and two other Oglala chiefs came to Walsh and told him the same thing.

Never had Sitting Bull so defiantly challenged the authority of Major Walsh, certainly not to the edge of violence. Never had he so openly defied the White Mother's laws and rules. If he was thinking clearly, he must have understood that he was risking his chance to remain free in Canada. But the old warrior's temper was up. He doubtless felt humiliated to have backed down while his people watched.

For his part, Major Walsh handled the crisis with courage if not good judgment. He told a watching newsman that he knew the time had come when he must completely cow Sitting Bull or lose all control over the Lakotas. He had made up his mind to arrest or kill Sitting Bull if he touched the horse again. He knew his command might be wiped out as they faced the Lakotas, "but we might as well be killed at once as to let the Tetons know we feared them."

In aiding One Bull instead of leaving him to face the consequences of his theft, Sitting Bull endangered his relationship with Major Walsh and the Mounted Police and even with the Canadian government. A day's reflection cooled his temper and made him understand the effect of his action. If Long Lance would pardon him, he could continue to live free in the White Mother's domain. Wisdom was one of the four cardinal virtues of Lakota manhood. To beg forgiveness, Sitting Bull would show the wisdom required to heal a potentially fatal breach with Major Walsh. Sitting Bull returned to Wood Mountain Post, apologized to Major Walsh, and begged his forgiveness, which was granted.⁴

Major Walsh failed to display the wisdom of Sitting Bull. That he was ready, even only said he was ready, to kill Sitting Bull and sacrifice his own life and that of his entire command belies his sterling record as a policeman. Rarely had he lost his temper in dealing with Sitting Bull, although he had ample provocation. But his statement was made in the heat of the moment. It is hard to picture him shooting Sitting Bull or any other Indian except in self-defense.

In any event, the episode passed without leaving any apparent rancor.

Walsh and Sitting Bull were friends. Walsh loved to be known as "Sitting Bull's boss." But as neither boss nor friend had he been able to convince Sitting Bull to return to his homeland. Other Hunkpapa chiefs, emboldened by Sitting Bull's lifting of his ban on surrender, had begun moving south. Why not Sitting Bull? And why, after a year, did the defectors again risk "soldiering" by the akicita? The akicita had kept Sitting Bull's following from defecting for the first three years in Canada. Now, with his following dwindling, Sitting Bull had reimposed the ban to maintain a substantial enough following to respect him as chief.

Major Walsh was not without enemies or detractors among the officers of the Mounted Police. Many were motivated by jealousy and others offended by his arrogance, his vanity, and his openly displayed ambition. He was not above conniving politically to get his way. Some wrote critical letters to higher authority and to other officers. But none, high or low, questioned his influence on Sitting Bull.

The thought occurred to Sir John A. Macdonald, former premier and now Canada's minister of the interior, that Walsh's influence prevented Sitting Bull from leaving—indeed, that Walsh was actively encouraging him to stay. That was not true, although Walsh's friendship and sympathy may have combined with the other factors that in Sitting Bull's mind prevented surrender.

Walsh was due to depart on six-month leave on July 15, 1880. Shortly before departing he received orders to take command of Fort Qu'Appelle, 140 miles northeast of Wood Mountain. On his return from leave, that would be his station. And that presumably would separate him from Sitting Bull.[5]

On July 6 Walsh met with Sitting Bull on the subject of surrender and several days later with Big Road and the leading Oglala chiefs. They all said they would surrender if Walsh would go to Washington and talk with the American president in their behalf. They wanted a reservation at the head of Tongue River or to be allowed to live with the Yanktonais at the Fort Peck Agency at Poplar on the Missouri River. Walsh said that if Ottawa consented he would travel to Washington and talk with the president.[6]

Walsh kept his promise, with results he must have anticipated. In Ottawa Interior Minister Macdonald forbade his trying to see the president in Washington. At his home in Brockville, Ontario, on September 9, Walsh wrote a long letter to Macdonald setting forth his thoughts on Sitting Bull.

Sitting Bull's first request to Walsh was that he try to get the Canadian government to accept him as a subject and permit him to enjoy all the benefits of native Canadian tribes. This would allow him to live his traditional free life as a hunter as long as the buffalo lasted.

His second request was that, if denied his first request by the Canadian government, Walsh would go to Washington, talk with the president, and learn the best terms on which his surrender would be received. Walsh thinks Sitting Bull believes he would be harshly treated if he surrendered without such assurances. Walsh wrote that he believed that if commitments could be made by the president or secretary of the interior, together with a few minor concessions, he could convince Sitting Bull to surrender.

Walsh added that Sitting Bull should not be given a reservation in Canada. He believed that Sitting Bull's ambition was too great to allow him to settle down and pursue the free life without followers to lead. His presence would make trouble with native Canadians and be a magnet drawing disaffected American tribesmen from below the border. Walsh's assessment of Sitting Bull explained these reasons and revealed the roots of the bonds of friendship that had flowered:

> In my opinion he is the shrewdest and most intelligent Indian living, has the ambition of Napoleon, and is brave to a fault. He is respected as well as feared by every Indian on the plains. In war he has no equal. In council he is superior to all. Every word said by him carries weight, and is quoted and passed from camp to camp.[7]

Walsh's evaluation of Sitting Bull is that of the only white man to gain his trust and friendship. He doubtless regarded himself as the most qualified person to represent Sitting Bull's interests to the American president. In Ottawa he had been forcefully told that he could not go to Washington. In his letter he implied that he stood ready to do so. In Washington, however, the diplomats were still striving for a solution to the Sitting Bull problem. Walsh was a policeman of relatively low rank, and his intervention in the diplomats' business would be certain to cause trouble. The Sitting Bull problem had become an international problem, one to be handled by diplomats, not soldiers. Besides, Walsh understood that his friendship with Sitting Bull had been the reason for isolating him from Sitting Bull.

Removing Major Walsh from Wood Mountain did not solve the problem. Sitting Bull continued to delay a decision because Walsh had told him to take no action until he returned from leave, or in another version until the first snow fell.

But Walsh simply could not let go, just as Sitting Bull could not let go. Four years of fruitful cooperation bound them together.

As a consequence of Walsh's transfer to Qu'Appelle, Sitting Bull had to deal with new officers. The sternest and most difficult was Walsh's successor at Wood Mountain: Maj. Leif Newby Fitzroy Crozier, "Paddy" to his comrades. Some associates regarded him as the most competent officer in the force, but his successes alternated with failures.

A new police commissioner was appointed in November 1880. Lt. Col. Acheson G. Irvine was a competent officer with a stern face and full beard, less inclined than Crozier to treat Indians harshly. He at once took on the Sitting Bull problem. From his headquarters at Fort Walsh, he journeyed over to Wood Mountain often enough to be named "Big Bull" by the Lakotas. He met with Sitting Bull and his headmen at Wood Mountain on November 23, 1880. Irvine asked Sitting Bull if Walsh had ever held forth the possibility of obtaining a reserve in Canada. Sitting Bull did not answer the question until Irvine pressed him again. Finally, he said that Walsh had gone to see the Queen and the president of the United States and that he would return and tell him what to do.

Irvine could get nothing more from Sitting Bull but requests to send for Walsh, as he could do nothing until he saw Walsh. As he explained:

When Walsh was here, I told him I did not know what to do. I was like a bird on the fence, not knowing on what side to hop. I mean on which side of the line to live. I was inclined to surrender to the United States. He told me to wait here in Canada until he returned, and he would then tell me what to do.

Repeatedly Irvine told Sitting Bull that Walsh would not return to Wood Mountain. Sitting Bull then said that Walsh had told him that the government was building houses for him in the north (Fort Qu'Appelle) and that if Walsh had not returned to Wood Mountain by the time the first snow fell, Sitting Bull was to go to Qu'Appelle to see him.[8]

An official of the ministry of the interior, Controller Frederick White, accompanied Irvine to Wood Mountain. He discovered that Walsh had sent tobacco to a trader to pass on to Sitting Bull as a pledge of good faith in carrying out his promises. If Walsh communicated with Wood Mountain as much as he had during his previous leave of absence, he kept in touch with Sitting Bull with more than a pouch of tobacco. White also wrote to Sir John about the "dishonest representations made to Sitting Bull by Superintendent Walsh, all calculated to lead to the belief that Superintendent Walsh, and he alone, was the man with whom Sitting Bull generally dealt."

Plainly, despite his removal from command at Wood Mountain Post, Major Walsh continued to influence Sitting Bull. And plainly Sitting Bull welcomed that influence. It gave him an excuse for putting off a decision on what to do.

The Mounted Police were not the only men trying to get Sitting Bull to surrender. The Americans were making a substantial effort. Frontiersman Edward H. Allison was the emissary. He had been a resident of the Upper Missouri for many years, an army scout, an agency interpreter, trader, and stockman. He was a longtime friend of Chief Gall, a big, powerful warrior who held high rank in the Hunkpapa tribe and had been close to Sitting Bull since childhood. The Indians called Allison "Fish."

In September 1880 Fish Allison arrived at Fort Buford after having helped drive a herd of cattle from the upper Milk River. En route he had met some Hunkpapa hunters and renewed his friendship with Gall. By the time he reached Fort Buford, he had decided that he could persuade Sitting Bull to surrender. He presented his plan to the post commander, Maj. David H. Brotherton, who eagerly accepted. General Terry approved on October 15.[9]

Major Brotherton would play a key role in the life of Sitting Bull throughout the rest of his months of freedom. A mature, thoughtful forty-eight years old, he had graduated from West Point in 1854 and spent virtually all of his career as an infantry officer in all parts of the West. In the Civil War in the Southwest, he earned a brevet for heroism in the Battle of Valverde. After the war he had served at several posts in the central Plains before assuming command of Fort Buford in 1880.

By time General Terry approved his mission, Allison had already completed the first of three missions. He had left Poplar River on October 1 and in two days found Sitting Bull on the southern edge of Wood Mountain just south of the boundary. His friend Gall welcomed him, but Sitting Bull would not meet or talk with him. He passed three days in Gall's lodge while urging surrender on all who would listen. Gall even pledged to take his entire following out of Sitting Bull's village and journey to Fort Buford.[10]

Allison embarked on his second expedition on October 24. He found Sitting Bull's camp at the mouth of Frenchmen's Creek, where it empties into Milk River. Again Gall greeted him warmly, and this time Sitting Bull asked him to join him in his lodge. For three days the Lakotas had been under attack by Blackfeet warriors seeking to steal horses. Each foray was driven off, but the fights left the Lakotas so unsettled that Allison had a hard time keeping their attention. In council Allison explained the terms on which they would be received. They were the same that had prevailed from the beginning: surrender arms and horses and settle at a U.S. agency. Sitting Bull rose to say that he knew the time had come when it was necessary for him to reach an understanding with the U.S. government, but he objected to the word "surrender." He was not in arms against the United States. In fact, he had never done more than defend himself against U.S. troops when hunting buffalo in his own country. And he had never relinquished his claim to that country, but was driven from it by force of arms; he wanted to be paid for it. Now the scarcity of game was a fact he could not overlook. Major Walsh had told him that he would return and act as mediator between him and all white men and had urged Sitting Bull to make no agreements until his return. He intended to keep that promise.[11]

Gall was more receptive. During Allison's first visit he had promised to arrange the surrender of the entire band. He had not accomplished that, but he did persuade twenty families to accompany him as a token of good faith. They went as far as Poplar before stopping to wait for Sitting Bull.

At Fort Keogh Bear Coat Miles was holding about one thousand Lakotas who had surrendered. He still obsessed about Sitting Bull, and early in October he dispatched scout W. E. Everette to locate Sitting Bull and order him to surrender within thirty days or Miles would lead an expedition against him. Everette returned with Sitting Bull's answer: he would not give a positive answer until he heard from Major Walsh.[12]

Back at Fort Buford, on November 7 Allison informed Major Brotherton that if the Lakotas could get no meat, he believed that they would come to Fort Buford and talk about surrender.[13]

Allison's third journey to Sitting Bull began on November 14. He was at Wood Mountain on November 22. Colonel Irvine, the new chief of the Mounted Police, was also there to impress on Sitting Bull the urgency of surrender. Sitting Bull answered that he was ready to surrender at Fort Buford, but could not say exactly when. The weather was very cold, and he did not know all the things he would have to do in preparation. Allison attributed the present delay to a "lingering hope" that Walsh would return. From what Allison could learn, he was certain that Major Walsh had been in communication with Sitting Bull since his departure.[14]

Fish Allison prevailed. On December 10 he dispatched a courier to Major Brotherton with word that he would start the next morning with Sitting Bull and his entire camp, more than one hundred lodges. The Indians were poor and had little food and only a few ponies, so in the freezing weather they would move slowly. Ten days would take them only to the mouth of Milk River, where it flowed into the Missouri. They would have to stop there to hunt buffalo. Allison also worried that the buffalo might stampede. At the Poplar Agency many Indians camped awaiting the process of surrender. Troops and restless "hostiles" made a volatile combination. As Allison advised Brotherton by courier, "Indians are like so many wild cattle—the least thing would excite or stampede them. . . . A premature movement of troops would bring about the very catastrophe which we wish to avoid."[15]

The only troops to worry about were two companies of infantry under Capt. Ogden B. Read, sent to Poplar by General Terry to keep order among the fractious Lakotas at the agency. However, on December 25 Maj. Guido Ilges arrived with nearly four hundred soldiers of the Fifth Infantry from Fort Keogh and established camp at Poplar

Agency. Miles was no longer to be contended with. At last he had been promoted to brigadier general and had left on a new assignment.[16]

In obtaining Sitting Bull's agreement to surrender, Edward Allison had accomplished more than Walsh or any other Canadian officer assigned the task. But he had not yet got them to Fort Buford to surrender. And the "premature movement of troops" that worried Allison was about to happen.

Montana's Poplar River agency lay on the north bank of the Missouri River sixty miles downstream from the mouth of the Milk, where Sitting Bull camped. It served as the agency for the Yanktonai Indians. But in December 1880 it also hosted many Indians in addition to the resident Yanktonais. Most were Hunkpapas who had left Sitting Bull with the intent to surrender. For many the intent had weakened. They could not surrender at Poplar because the government had designated Forts Keogh and Buford as the places to surrender. The leading chiefs were Gall and Crow King, both Hunkpapas close to Sitting Bull.

Gall had temporized about surrendering, but by the end of December he and the other chiefs were ready. They said they did not want to go to Buford now; it was too cold for the women and children. They would decide when to go. Ilges pressed them and finally provoked them into declaring that they would fight before they would expose their people to subzero temperatures. That was understandable. Temperatures ran as low as thirty below with snow several feet deep.

Ilges took the attitude of the Lakotas as an invitation to fight. On January 2, 1881, Ilges fought, although it was a one-sided fight. The major trained his single artillery piece on the Lakota tipis, pitched in brushy timber in the river valley and sheltering about three hundred people. The exploding shells quickly flattened some tipis and brought forth a waving white flag of surrender. Lakota casualties were one dead and one wounded. The rest scattered, most heading for a Yanktonai camp up the river. The soldiers burned the tipis.[17]

The Ilges fight was exactly what Fish Allison had feared. Gall and the others forced to surrender were dispatched to Fort Buford. It was a grueling trip in the fierce weather that had led the Indians to provoke Ilges by refusing to leave until conditions moderated. Ilges prepared to march upriver to Sitting Bull's village. Allison had already set forth upriver, and on January 21 he met Good Bear with fifty-one lodges and seventy families. They had broken away from Sitting Bull and were on their way to surrender. That left Sitting Bull with about 150 warriors in fifty lodges. Allison sent Hunkpapa couriers to reassure Sitting Bull and continued to his village.

But on January 10 Allison received orders from Terry to suspend his talks with Sitting Bull. Terry felt that Sitting Bull was using one pretext after another to delay coming to Buford. As soon as Allison had carried out those instructions, he was to hasten back to Poplar and inform Major Ilges, who then would march up the river to attack Sitting Bull. The attack did not happen. Sitting Bull and the remnant of his following were no longer at Milk River but moving north to return to Canada and Wood Mountain.[18]

Fort Buford continued to hum with activity as Major Brotherton and Fish Allison sought the surrender of Sitting Bull. They both knew that, in numbers large and small, starving Lakotas were breaking away from the chief and heading for Buford, which already cared for eleven hundred surrendered Indians. On February 6 Crow King, Sitting Bull's head soldier, arrived at Buford with 352 Lakotas and turned in their firearms. These people had been part of Sitting Bull's following at the mouth of Milk River and had departed over strenuous objections. Crow King said that Sitting Bull would have to come in because small groups continued to desert him. To encourage further breakaways, with the aid of Crow King Major Brotherton selected four Hunkpapas, one Crow King's brother, to go to Sitting Bull and explain the situation at Fort Buford to him and his remaining people.[19]

With seventy-six lodges, Sitting Bull arrived at Wood Mountain on January 31, 1881, and pitched camp three miles from the Mounted Police post. The Lakotas had almost no food, and their clothing was in rags. They did have many horses and 150 buffalo robes. Both horses and robes were quickly traded to the Wood Mountain traders.[20]

Sitting Bull explained to Major Crozier why he had come back to Wood Mountain instead of surrendering as so many of his people had:

> I do not believe the Americans, they are liars in everything. They like to be in touch with the Indians to make money. I went towards the agency against my will because the Great Mother told me to go. I knew all the time the Americans would not tell the truth and when I took one step forward I stopped to think before going on again. I have shown you that they are untruthful and I have come back here and I am going to remain to raise my children.[21]

But many of his people had surrendered, and in small groups they continued to surrender. His following dwindled perilously. The redcoats no longer treated him kindly. In council, Major Crozier ignored him and spoke to the entire group. Col. "Big Bull" Irvine, the chief of the Mounted Police, rode over from Fort Walsh with increasing frequency to pressure Sitting Bull into giving up. As he had so often before, Sitting Bull fell into the mood of not knowing what to do—as he had once said, on which side of the fence to jump.

6

Indecision

Sitting Bull did not know what to do. Colonel Irvine, the "Big Bull" who commanded the North-West Mounted Police, often came from Fort Walsh and met with him to insist with increasing fervor that he take his people to Fort Buford, Dakota, and surrender to Maj. David H. Brotherton. There most of the other Hunkpapas who had surrendered were being held until melting ice opened the Missouri River for steamboats to take them to their agency. Sitting Bull was told that they were well fed and cared for, but he did not believe it. To remain in Canada, however, inevitably meant starvation. He desperately longed to see Major Walsh.

Major Crozier, the Wood Mountain commander, met with Sitting Bull more often than Irvine and said the same thing, although more emphatically. Unlike Major Walsh, Crozier was not friendly with Sitting Bull. In fact, he adopted a deliberately unfriendly approach in hopes of undermining Sitting Bull's ascendancy:

> I therefore concluded to break his influence with the camp; consequently, on subsequent occasions instead of treating him with exceptional deference and addressing myself especially to him in council, I spoke to the people generally, telling them not to allow any one or any set of men to prevent them from accepting the American terms of surrender. I explained how much their women and children would benefit by such a step; that whatever they as men thought, or whatever prejudices any particular man had respecting the Americans, they would be cruel to their families if

they longer rejected the offer, now that starvation was imminent in this country and that they could not now hunt south of the line without a constant dread of attack from the American troops.

Crozier's bullying may have had an effect, for he reported that soon after he adopted this approach groups began to leave. Sitting Bull used One Bull's akicita to prevent defections, sometimes by force.[1]

Sitting Bull had few choices before him. He could remain indecisive at Wood Mountain in the hope that Major Walsh would come as promised and tell him what to do. He could go north to Fort Qu'Appelle, Walsh's new station, and meet him there when he returned from leave. Walsh had told him to do that if he had not come to Wood Mountain by the first snow. But winter was almost over; this was spring 1881. The snows were melting, and Walsh had not come. Should he go to Fort Qu'Appelle, he might still find Walsh because he commanded the post.

Or he could go east thirty-five miles to Willow Bunch, where his friend Jean Louis Legaré had moved his trading post from Wood Mountain in 1880. Jean Louis sometimes gave Sitting Bull's people food. Maybe he would now that they were hungry and sick. Unknown to Sitting Bull, Crozier had written to Jean Louis asking him to try to get the Hunkpapas to go to Fort Buford, which meant sharing some of his food if necessary. (Willow Bunch was also known as Little Wood Mountain, and in common usage the two often became confused. Documents using the term Wood Mountain, for example, often meant Willow Bunch.)

Despite the pressures of Colonel Irvine and Major Crozier on Sitting Bull, and the looming likelihood of starvation, he could not bring himself to decide the fate of his own life and his people's. Both to Walsh and his successors, he had voiced the fear that he would be badly treated at Fort Buford. If not hanged for his role in the Custer disaster, he would be imprisoned. The latest rumor was that the Hunkpapas at Fort Buford were being held in irons. His fears were not eased when four Hunkpapas arrived at Wood Mountain from Fort Buford with the explicit mission of painting an appealing picture.

On General Terry's suggestion, early in February 1881 Major Brotherton had selected four men from Crow King's band to journey to Wood Mountain, explain to Sitting Bull how well his people were treated at Fort Buford, and try to induce him to return with them and surrender. They spent the last half of March on this mission and succeeded in convincing twenty-nine lodges, about two hundred people, to head south and surrender, but not Sitting Bull. He remained with about forty lodges, still undecided even in the face of death by starvation, which he had seen too often that winter.[2]

On April 3 Sitting Bull asked to meet privately with Major Crozier. The Hunkpapas that Major Brotherton had sent had broken off nearly half of his following, but they had failed to convince Sitting Bull of the true conditions at Fort Buford, which were good. "I do not believe everything the Indians who were here the other day said," he informed Crozier. He had been told that Lakotas who had surrendered were held in chains, and he feared the same treatment for himself if he surrendered. He still needed to be convinced of conditions at Fort Buford, and he had a proposal for Crozier. Sitting Bull would send two of his young men on whom he could rely to Fort Buford. "I want these two young men to go that they may see for themselves how the Americans are treating the Indians and then they will return and tell me everything. Send one of your men with them so that he too may see everything for I know what a redcoat says is true."[3]

Crozier interpreted this to mean that Sitting Bull had finally made a decision, although the mission to Fort Buford was intended to lead him to make this decision. Quoting Sitting Bull, Crozier wrote, "Tell the Americans not to be afraid that I will eat the little provisions they send me and then not go in. They will see me. They may say if he wants our food let him come and get it. They will see me soon. I have given my word and my body to the Queen and will do what I am told. I am in earnest. I am going in." Crozier passed this on the Brotherton.[4]

These words ring of authenticity. Crozier could not have made them up or gilded Sitting Bull's words so expansively. As he had demonstrated in the past, Sitting Bull held the Queen in great esteem. If she wanted him to go back to his homeland, he believed he should go. And he seems to have said so in unmistakable terms. There is no reason to doubt that at this moment he intended to go. But he had a record of changing his mind, or of imagining circumstances that undermined such pronouncements. Otherwise, why allow the mission he had arranged with Major Crozier when these words appeared to make it unnecessary? He allowed the delegation to Fort Buford to proceed. At least it would buy time for further thought.

If the three men, including a redcoat, returned with a favorable report, he would feel more secure in carrying out his stated intent. Sitting Bull named to the group his always reliable nephew, One Bull, and Bone Club, a son of Four Horns. Crozier assigned Capt. Alexander Macdonell, his executive officer. At Poplar, en route to Buford, Macdonell handed Captain Read a letter from Crozier stating that his mission was to "arrange for the surrender of Sitting Bull," and at Fort Buford, where the delegation arrived on April 9, he delivered a letter from Crozier stating that Sitting Bull would "in all probability" surrender once the Macdonell party returned. Macdonell told Major Brotherton that, for the first time, Sitting Bull had said he would come in, that he had given his word to the Queen. Crozier appeared highly sanguine that Sitting Bull at last had decided.

Brotherton let the delegation mingle with the surrendered Indians, now about eleven hundred in number. They were scattered in tipis and army tents on the bottoms facing the Missouri River across from the mouth of the Yellowstone River, and some were housed in an army warehouse. They had been provided with stoves and fuel, warm clothing, blankets, and as much food as they wanted. They told the emissaries that they were well and courteously cared for and were glad they had come to Buford. As the delegation prepared to depart on April 12, Major Brotherton threw a farewell feast in the post mess hall.[5]

The delegation returned to Wood Mountain on April 17. Sitting Bull organized a council to hear what they had to say. Crozier handed Sitting Bull a letter from Major Brotherton describing conditions at the fort, which Crozier read. He also presented some tobacco and a blanket as peace offerings from Brotherton. Macdonell followed with his own observation of what he had seen and heard. He said that the prisoners were not restricted to a ration but got all they could eat and were well clothed. The record does not disclose what One Bull and Bone Club said. But Sitting Bull said simply that he had nothing to say. Why? Eight years later Macdonell recalled that the Indians who went with him did not favor surrender and therefore lied about what they had seen. If the two Indians contributed nothing, One Bull would have communicated his observations to his uncle in private, and it is unlikely that he would have lied. The truth is probably that Sitting Bull had once more slipped into his mood of indecision.[6]

That very afternoon more of Sitting Bull's people began pulling down their lodges and packing to move. They said they were going to Willow Bunch, where some Lakotas had preceded them, but Crozier believed that Sitting Bull still intended to go to Qu'Appelle. Crozier wrote to ask Jean Louis Legaré, who drew his stock from Buford traders, to take with him on his next journey any Lakotas who could be induced to surrender.[7]

Sitting Bull had made another, more ominous decision. He had decided that his following had diminished so much, especially in young fighting men, that he could not defend himself against the aggressions of the Canadian Crees and Blackfeet, who repeatedly raided his horse herds. The need for more warriors was especially pressing because his people were strung out moving by groups to Willow Bunch. Sixty lodges remained at Wood Mountain, sixteen were at Willow Bunch, and thirty to forty were en route to Willow Bunch. Sitting Bull resolved to entice warriors who had surrendered to rejoin him. He sent runners to Fort Buford with tobacco and an appeal to break free and return to him in Canada. Such was his prestige that, despite the scarcity of buffalo, the free life in Canada under their great chief Sitting Bull seemed superior to the life at Standing Rock Agency, to which steamboats would soon transport them. Even so, not many left the comforts of Fort Buford. For one thing, on recommendation of Fish Allison, the scout who had tried to get Sitting Bull to surrender, Running Antelope had been brought up from Standing Rock Agency. Known for his bravery in war and skills in oratory and diplomacy, Running Antelope was one of four Hunkpapa principal chiefs who acted as close advisors to Sitting Bull. His belief that compromise with the whites was in their best interests led to his eventually distancing himself from Sitting Bull. At the Standing Rock Reservation everyone liked him, and he used his influence to prevent defections.[8]

Sitting Bull's foreboding proved correct only two days after the Macdonell party had returned from Buford. On the morning of April 18 a Lakota woman spotted a Cree warrior hiding in the brush and gave the alarm. As the men searched the brush, the Cree ran to the gate of the fort and entered. After discovering where the Cree was, an angry Sitting Bull, backed by some of his men, met Crozier at the gate, demanded the Cree, and tried to push his way in. Crozier shoved him aside, closed the gate, and put his men under arms. Crozier then went out of the gate and confronted Sitting Bull. Sitting Bull explained that the Cree was one of a party of Crees that had stolen some Lakota horses during the night, and he wanted the Cree surrendered. Crozier told him that, if he came to him in a rational manner, he would investigate, but he would not be intimidated. Sitting Bull and his men sat down in a sullen mood and remained until Four Horns proposed that they smoke a peace pipe. After completing the pipe ceremony, the men again sat and brooded until they saw that they could not have their way. Then they dispersed.[9]

According to Major Crozier, Sitting Bull was terrified at the prospect of fighting off Canadian Indians, whose resentment of the foreign Lakotas deepened with the decline of the buffalo. Even then a war party of two hundred Crees and Blackfeet was said to be on its way to Wood Mountain intent on killing Sitting Bull. His young warriors, who would have to fight off these Canadian Indians, were slipping away to surrender. At the end of March the influential Oglala war chief Low Dog and his people, about two hundred crowded into twenty lodges, had defected, depriving Sitting Bull of fifty young men.[10]

Five hundred Hunkpapas, including all the important chiefs, reached Willow Bunch on April 20 in their usual impoverished condition—ragged clothing, hardly any food, all possessions deteriorating. Jean Louis lectured them sternly about the certainty of starvation if they remained in Canada and urged them to accompany him on his next trip to Buford for supplies.[11]

On April 28, three days after Jean Louis's advice-laden feast, Sitting Bull and twenty lodges packed and moved north on the road to Qu'Appelle, 150 miles away. Most who went with him were old men, women, and children, but a half-dozen high-ranking chiefs went too, among them Four Horns, No Neck, and Iron Star, and some young men. Sitting Bull's overriding reason for the journey was to see Major Walsh and learn what he should do. He would wait at Qu'Appelle until Walsh returned from the East.[12]

Walsh's leave had been for six months. He had now been absent for nine months, and presumably Interior Minister Macdonald would ensure that he remained absent until Sitting Bull surrendered. Still, that Sitting Bull clung to the fantasy of Walsh's return and would journey to Qu'Appelle in hopes of seeing him testifies to the trust and friendship he reposed in this man of another race, a man that he looked on as a friend.

By this time Walsh suspected that the government would ensure that he never again saw Sitting Bull. Even so, he felt an obligation to this chief of towering prestige. He could simply have remained distant and let others deal with Sitting Bull. But he took action. He traveled to New York and Chicago and looked up old friends who had political influence. One such, Indian Bureau Inspector J. H. Hammond, explored the question and assured Walsh that Sitting Bull could surrender in safety. He would be welcomed and forgiven any atrocities that authorities believed he had committed, including the Little Bighorn. Walsh also had friends with influence in the president's cabinet. They said that, if Sitting Bull surrendered and was not cordially treated, they would intervene on his behalf. Walsh then enlisted Louis Daniels, a former policeman who had served with him on the force and who was acquainted with Sitting Bull. Daniels was then en route to Qu'Appelle himself. Walsh asked him to find Sitting Bull and assure him, in Walsh's name, that he could surrender and he would receive the same treatment as Big Road, Gall, Spotted Eagle, and others, all of whom had received kind treatment.[13]

This word from Walsh via Louis Daniels was not the same as receiving it directly from Walsh, and Fort Qu'Appelle was the place to meet with Walsh. Walsh knew this. "I know Bull thoroughly," he told a Toronto newsman, "and am satisfied he has no intention of returning to U.S. territory until he sees me. Bull knows that I am to come back in the course of time, and although my command [Fort Qu'Appelle] is two hundred miles from his camp [at Wood Mountain], I do not think very many days will elapse before Bull will make his appearance there." Apparently the records still bore Walsh's name as commander of Fort Qu'Appelle, and his words indicate that he thought he would return there. If so, he was blind to government policy or felt no remorse in challenging it—a trait that kept him in trouble as long as he remained in the Mounted Police.[14]

Qu'Appelle was a new but growing town south of a broad valley containing a long string of lakes. The lakes were carved by several rivers draining rolling plains and timbered hills. It owed its origins to the Hudson's Bay Company, whose abandoned fort stood on the hills above the largest lake. A Mounted Police station lay downstream in the village of Fort Qu'Appelle, where the Indian Affairs office was also located. The Qu'Appelle area formed the stage on which Sitting Bull dealt with another branch of Canadian officialdom, the Office of Indian Affairs.

The Indians had raised their lodges in several camps on hills south of the Qu'Appelle Valley, near the abandoned Hudson's Bay Company post. They were, as always, impoverished and hungry. The lake yielded fish and ducks. These afforded a spartan diet but not the traditional buffalo meat. They would live on this fare until more game could be found.

Shortly, they found some. A Catholic priest, Father Hugounard, presided over a mission four miles east of Fort Qu'Appelle. After a long winter his stores were depleted, and he sent to Fort Ellice for flour. Four carts returned with twenty-four hundred-pound bags of flour. The day after their arrival, the priest heard the sound of Indians singing. He watched the approach of a band of about seventy-five Lakota warriors, mounted, painted, befeathered, and chanting. They gave three loud whoops, tied their horses to the fence and came toward Hugounard's house. The one in the lead, still mounted, was Sitting Bull. After a warm exchange of "How, How, Cola," Hugounard sent for an interpreter. As all settled outside to wait, the priest gave them tobacco to smoke while he cooked dried buffalo meat and bacon. After the feasting ended, the interpreter arrived.

Hugounard asked Sitting Bull if he wanted to talk. Sitting Bull stood, shook hands with Hugounard, and spoke. The buffalo were gone, and they had come here to fish. But food was still scarce, and they were reduced to eating gophers and wild turnips. Sitting Bull could stand up to his enemies, he said, but not to children crying of hunger. The people had heard that Hugounard had flour, and he had come here to ask for part of it.

Yes, he had flour, Hugounard replied, and he would share it with people who needed it. But, he said, the Indians might have valuable items to exchange for it. The Indians applauded, and Sitting Bull took the blanket from around himself and presented it to Hugounard. Others gave five horses, and still others handed him artifacts gathered from the Little Bighorn, such as watches, saddles, and items of apparel. Hugounard gave them eight bags of flour, ammunition, dry goods, tea, and all the vegetables left over from winter, but he would not accept the plunder taken from the soldiers.[15]

Thanks to the priest, Sitting Bull and his people could for a time vary their diet of fish with bread made with the flour. But the greater possibility lay with the officer they now confronted: Edgar Dewdney, superintendent general of Indian affairs of the North-West Territories. He had been alerted by Ottawa to the coming of Sitting Bull and intended to meet with him.

On May 25 Indians from the nearest camp came down the lakeshore and approached Dewdney. They wanted to talk. Dewdney had hired the best interpreter in the vicinity and faced them. The leader was named Wachapi, probably one of Sitting Bull's headmen, and they wanted to talk because they were hungry. They had come a long way and they wanted a meal. Dewdney replied that from what he had heard from Wood Mountain, the government felt that it had been deceived and had instructed him to give them no assistance. That was true, Wachapi said, but they wanted one meal. Dewdney noted that Sitting Bull was not present and told the group to return at three o'clock in the afternoon with Sitting Bull.[16]

At the appointed hour, with Sitting Bull in charge, they crowded into the Indian Affairs office at Fort Qu'Appelle. One Bull was there, as was Sitting Bull's young son Crow Foot, named for the Blackfeet chief with whom he had made peace. Sitting Bull now spoke for everyone except Four Horns, whom he said had not arrived yet. Dewdney began by telling Sitting Bull that he had a letter from Major Crozier describing Sitting Bull's bad behavior at Wood Mountain. Sitting Bull said that it was true, then added "I have not much to say now. I gave Major Walsh my fine clothing and told him to speak for me and that is what I am waiting for."

Dewdney asked if Colonel Irvine and Major Crozier had not advised him to surrender in his own country because Canada could not care for him and his people. Sitting Bull said that the Queen had told him to go back, but when he went last Christmas he was fired on by American soldiers and hastened back—a reference to the chaos that gripped Poplar at the end of 1880. Next, distorting reality, he proclaimed:

> I had not given up my country. I was only visiting it, and was coming back to see what Major Walsh had to send me. When I send any word I want it to be understood and I wanted to get an answer from Major Walsh. Since I am on this side of the line I liked to talk plain talk so that I might be understood when I came back to this side again. I told Col Irvine and Capt Crozier I want to get an answer from Major Walsh. I said what is the reason you are in such a hurry to send me across the line, what is the reason,

this is my country here, what is the reason you want to push me out of my country? You were from across the water. I thought you had come here to make money and feed those that were hungry, how is it that you are in a hurry to push me aside? I told him (Col Irvine) it is for the sake of our queen that you are here and my hands are tied and I do not intend to do anything wrong. I have received nothing in comparison with what the Crees have. The Great Spirit who made me made all upon this earth and made us that we eat buffalo meat. I told Col Irvine that the Great Spirit did not make me to live on the Half Breed and white man. This is the first time I have asked for assistance. I shake hands with the white man on this side and I feel safe. I shake hands with the Americans and am afraid of them. I told Capt Crozier no one has harmed me since I came on this side. I said how many times you ever hear of anyone fighting me on the Queen's ground. When I came across the line I came to live on this side with no evil intentions. I asked him who it was that spilt blood on that side of the line. I said what is the reason you are in such a hurry to send me away. I am waiting for an answer from Major Walsh and I am going to Qu'Appelle so I came away then.

The startling part of this rambling address came near the end. "Let us take ten chiefs from Canada and ten from America, ten of my people, ten of the Crees, ten priests and let us see who would be in the wrong after we had done talking." Whether he really believed that such a scheme could be arranged and carried out is questionable. He may have thought the omniscient Queen could do anything. Or he may have been simply stalling for time, to permit Major Walsh to return.

Commissioner Dewdney had come to Qu'Appelle to present to Sitting Bull and his people a plan formulated in Ottawa. If they refused to accept it, they would get no provisions or land from the government. For four years the Lakotas had been killing buffalo, and the Canadian Indians felt very unfriendly toward them. Several fights had taken place. The Canadian government could not control the Indians on the plains. This was a strong reason for accepting the government's plan. The same advice had been given by Colonel Macleod, Major Crozier, and other officers.

The government's offer was to provide daily rations to the Lakotas if they would return to the United States by moving down the Qu'Appelle River to the old Hudson's Bay post of Fort Ellice, at the mouth of the Assiniboine River, then turning southeast to the Red River, and entering the United States by way of the Red River and Pembina in Dakota. They would be met by American officers. Dewdney himself would accompany them to make sure they were properly treated by the Americans.

Such a plan was so elaborate that it required discussion by all in council. A council required food. The Indians only had a few ducks, not enough for the occasion. Dewdney supplied some food, and the council deliberated the next morning. In the afternoon Sitting Bull and twenty men assembled in the Indian office and met with Dewdney.

Sitting Bull took the floor at once and, avoiding the reason for the meeting, began pouring out words in great gushes, rambling from one subject to another. Finally he approached the matter he wanted to talk about. Colonel Irvine had come from Fort Walsh to Wood Mountain, Sitting Bull said, and told him that the Queen wanted him to go back and shake hands with the white man. He had, he explained, but the American soldiers had fired on his people and he had hastened back.

This was at best misleading. He was referring to the chaos at Poplar at the end of December 1880. Some of his people were indeed fired on, but not him or his immediate following. They were sixty miles up the Missouri River at the mouth of Milk River, and they had promptly returned to Canada. "I had not given up my country," he explained. "I was only visiting it, and was coming back to see what Major Walsh had to send to me."

He came to this country to make his home, he told Dewdney. He had sent word to the Queen that he wanted land like the Crees had, and she had not answered him in five years. The cruel, untrustworthy Americans had caused his people much suffering, and his people wanted to make their home in the Queen's land and enjoy the same advantages as the Crees, which meant rations to ward off hunger. He pointed to his five-year-old son Crow Foot. This was the first time he had brought Crow Foot to a council. Thereafter, it happened frequently, leading to the observation that he was "too smart and liked to give advice to his parents."[17]

Now, said Sitting Bull, "The child says to you, now Father look into this and find out where I may live a long time."

It is over five years since I sent my word to my Mother and I have heard no answer yet. Today my Mother the Queen will hear my words and I wonder what answer I am to get. The words I sent were these. I asked that there should be ten principal men of Sioux, Americans, priests, Canadians, Crees, and Half-Breeds (ten each) so they could talk it over and put everything straight. The reason why I sent this word was that it might be known who was in the wrong.

Dewdney wanted to know if this meant that he would he would go back to his homeland.

"Yes, that is what I said. That is the reason I asked you to give me something to eat. I know that the Americans are just waiting to hear my words. What our Mother the Queen said to me, I understand. I will go."

Dewdney asked if all his people said the same thing.

"Yes! Hear me! The heavens above hear me. They will all go as one man if I go. You want to know what is in my mind. I now let you know, and this is the first time I will let it be known. Now you know. And there is no one who wears the breech cloth that will go back on what I say. Now I want to know from you if the grub is going to be brought soon."

Dewdney replied that rations would be provided on the road down. Did he really mean what he had said?

"I meant that I would go down, if you could get the ten people asked for before to meet at Fort Garry [present Winnipeg] and settle what I want."

No, declared Dewdney. There was plenty of food at Fort Ellice, a journey of four days , and it would be provided once Sitting Bull agreed to return.

"If there was plenty there, why not send for it? I asked you to kill four animals, and you won't." Again, he said he wanted food, and again the answer was no.

Sitting Bull then said he was not so poor that he could not live, abruptly got up, and left the building, followed by his people.[18]

This was a prime example of Sitting Bull's resistance. The anticipated return of Major Walsh was another. But resistance was mixed with uncertainty about the future. For two years he had sought valid information on how he would be treated if he surrendered. Fort Buford held the surrendered Lakotas that winter, and repeated assurances of kind treatment failed to move him. In truth, the U.S. Army was anxious to get all the Lakotas onto their reservations and therefore treated them well at Fort Buford and Fort Keogh, where hundreds of others were held. It seems almost as if Sitting Bull did not want to believe in the favorable treatment reliably reported to him. So he continued to resist until surrender became the only course, and even then, on the way to surrender, he resisted.

This was a remarkable exchange between Sitting Bull and Commissioner Dewdney. But the strangest part of was the edict to assemble ten men from each of a specified category of people: Indians, Canadians, Americans, priests, half-breeds, and Crees. Could he have grasped how impossible it would be to gather such an array? Or what such a diverse gathering could accomplish even if assembled? Was he serious? Was he indulging in obfuscation of Dewdney? Was he simply raising an obstacle to returning to his homeland? Notably, this mandate, in vivid contrast to the rest of his diatribe, was clearly stated and seems to have been proposed before. It stood forth plainly amid an ocean of words.

Finally, it may indeed have made sense to him. The Indian way of decision-making was to assemble all parties to an issue and talk it over, everyone having a say before coming to a consensus. Moreover, the Indian way was to share food if it was available. Food was available, and Dewdney would not share.

If Sitting Bull's oratorical skills failed him, however, Dewdney could claim no better, although he could in large part blame Ottawa. The government's plan was deeply flawed. The "grub" was the only positive factor. To herd forty lodges of Indians down the Qu'Appelle and Assiniboine Rivers to enter the United States at Pembina, Dakota, was a massive undertaking. Commercial steamers plied the waterways, but contracting with the companies and boarding all these Indians and their possessions seems not to have been arranged or contemplated. The distance to Pembina was nearly six hundred miles. Even if they succeeded in getting them into Dakota, it was still 385 miles from Pembina to Fort Buford. And had Canadian authorities consulted with Americans to ensure that troops would be present to escort them to Fort Buford or the agencies to which their kinsmen had already been transported? If so, no evidence has been found.

One wonders what Dewdney would have done if Sitting Bull had accepted the government plan. It may not have been as unrealistic as Sitting Bull's demand for ten men from various groups to meet, but it would have been almost as difficult to carry out.

Much simpler and maybe even more realistic was Sitting Bull's intent to meet with Major Walsh, either at Qu'Appelle or Wood Mountain.

Wood Mountain was the destination when Sitting Bull and his people set forth from Qu'Appelle on June 16, 1881, leaving Edgar Dewdney to explain to the authorities in Ottawa as best he could his failure to rid Canada of Sitting Bull.

Another perspective emerged when a newsman met two discharged Mounted Police who had talked with Sitting Bull after the meeting with Dewdney. They said that Sitting Bull believed that Dewdney had no right to try to force the Lakotas to leave Canada. Their perspective showed what at least two of Walsh's troopers thought of their adversary:

> What we policemen thought was pretty hard was the fact that while many of us, who have known Sitting Bull personally and have partaken of his hospitality on many cold winter's night and when tired out with a hard march through the snow, we should now be ordered under severe penalty, not to give him or one of his tribe or children, so much as a biscuit or even to speak to them. He always used us square after he got to know us and many a time helped us with his braves in recovering stolen horses, cattle &c and we did not think it fair that we should be prevented from sharing our rations with one of his hungry tribe.[19]

Not all Canadians believed the government was handling the issue properly or fairly. Sitting Bull was a large issue throughout Canada, and citizens followed the story in their newspapers. As a citizen wrote to the editor of the *Toronto Globe*,

> Speculation is rife concerning the motives of the Government in preventing Major Walsh from meeting with Sitting Bull. Here is an officer in whom Sitting Bull is said to have implicit confidence, and who has the reputation of knowing thoroughly the Indian character with all its peculiarities, can talk their language, and is honest in his dealings with them to the last degree; and with all the apparent anxiety of the United States and Canadian Governments for this Indian chief's surrender, Major Walsh is kept in Ontario for many months (under pay) by the Canadian Government, away from his post in the North-West, where his presence would in all probability amicably settle matters. . . . Is it that the Government does not wish to treat Sitting Bull fairly, and Major Walsh, not wishing to deceive the old chief, refuses to return to his post, and meet with him?[20]

Maj. James M. Walsh had been a loyal friend of Sitting Bull's for four years, the only white man who could make that claim then and possibly ever. (In 1885 Buffalo Bill Cody may have earned that distinction.) Walsh, however, could no longer influence these events. Sitting Bull, continuing his resistance, did not know this. He still hoped for Walsh's return. While waiting, he would look to another man: Willow Bunch trader Jean Louis Legaré.

7

Jean Louis

Jean Louis Legaré—everyone called him Jean Louis, he said—had set up a trading post at Wood Mountain in 1871 to trade with the local settlement of Métis, an ethnic group that played a large role in Canadian history. He was thirty years old in 1871 and an impressive man—six feet four inches tall with a muscular physique and a full black beard, friendly, generous, competent.

Jean Louis had first met Sitting Bull six years after establishing his post at Wood Mountain, in May 1877, when he and his people received permission from Major Walsh to remain in Canada. Walsh had also allowed them to receive a small quantity of ammunition to enable them to hunt. Their own supplies were exhausted. The ammunition would come from Jean Louis's store.

The ammunition did indeed prove essential to avert hunger in the Indian camps. Moreover, it brought the Lakotas together with Jean Louis, with whom they traded until, faced with increasing competition from other traders, he moved his business to Willow Bunch in 1880. Willow Bunch was a small community thirty miles east of Wood Mountain. Jean Louis dealt with the Indians honestly and even generously. Occasionally, when hunger stalked the camps, he provided food. As the historian of Saskatchewan wrote, "The well-known fur trader, Louis Le Garé, of Willow Bunch, informs the writer that at his own expense he supported the starving Indians with a large amount of food, and that he had numerous serious conferences with Sitting Bull and his subordinates."[1]

Sitting Bull arrived at Willow Bunch with five hundred people on April 20, 1881. They were starving and told Jean Louis that Major Crozier had ordered them away from Wood Mountain Post after losing patience with them. Crozier had also written Jean Louis urging him to encourage the Lakotas to surrender. Any who agreed could go with him on his periodic trips to Fort Buford for merchandise. Fort Buford was where the surrendered Hunkpapas were being held through the winter, until the Missouri River ice thawed and allowed steamboats to resume operation. Jean Louis thought he could succeed in such a plan. It would cost a great deal of money because he would have to feed his charges while en route, but he believed that the U.S. government would reimburse him for his expenses.[2]

On April 25, five days after the Lakotas reached Willow Bunch, Jean Louis staged a feast. Besides Sitting Bull, all of his chiefs were present. Jean Louis told the assemblage that the Mounted Police had sent them away, that the Queen would not give them land in Canada, and that he was the only friend they had left. If they wanted their children to live longer, they would take Jean Louis's advice and go back to the other side of the boundary, where they would be issued rations. Sitting Bull spoke for the chiefs in saying that Jean Louis's word was good, but that they could not trust the Americans. Jean Louis countered that he made periodic trips to Fort Buford to obtain stock for his store. He would furnish carts and provisions for any who would accompany him to the fort. He would introduce them to the commanding officer, Maj. David H. Brotherton, and let them see how well their fellow tribesmen were treated. If Brotherton promised good treatment, Legaré reasoned, some of the Indians might surrender.

Sixteen of Sitting Bull's followers agreed to go. The journey required eight days to cover 150 miles and was made in Red River carts, big two-wheeled wagons pulled by teams of horses. At Fort Buford Jean Louis conferred with Major Brotherton about showing the delegation how they would be treated if they surrendered. If they were impressed, some or all might remain. He hoped that all would, but he would take back to Willow Bunch any who wished. Brotherton wanted to know why he wished to take any back. Because, replied

Legaré, Sitting Bull and his fellow chiefs were too suspicious to believe anyone but their own people. Twelve Lakotas chose to remain at Fort Buford, and four accompanied Jean Louis back to Willow Bunch, where they arrived on May 12.[3]

Old Bull was one of the Lakotas who chose to go with Jean Louis. He was Sitting Bull's brother-in-law but had been intrigued by Jean Louis's words about Fort Buford. He wanted to see for himself how Sitting Bull's people would be treated by the American soldiers. As he later remembered, at the fort he met with old friends and was impressed with what he heard and saw. They were contented and well fed. Old Bull carried a favorable story back for Sitting Bull.[4]

But Sitting Bull was not at Willow Bunch. Hoping to meet Major Walsh, he and twenty lodges had moved north on the road to Qu'Appelle, where instead of Walsh they collided with Indian Commissioner Edgar Dewdney (see chapter 6, above).

As Sitting Bull and his following made their way toward Qu'Appelle, Jean Louis prepared another caravan for Fort Buford. Four men, including Old Bull, had returned with him on the previous trip. Jean Louis held a council in which he had these four relate what they had seen at Fort Buford. They spoke so convincingly of good treatment that all the people were pleased and begged Jean Louis to delay the departure of his next journey until Sitting Bull had returned to help them decide. Jean Louis refused. He needed the merchandise awaiting him at Buford. But he invited all who wanted to go to climb on his carts for the trip. The Indians held another council to talk the issue over. When the caravan left, thirty-two climbed aboard.[5]

Among the thirty-two was Sitting Bull's sixteen-year-old daughter, Many Horses, an attractive and competent young lady, and her warrior paramour. The young man had gone to Sitting Bull and offered ten horses in payment for her hand. Sitting Bull had refused. Family meant a lot to him, and he would not part with his daughter. With her father absent en route to Qu'Appelle, however, the couple took advantage of Jean Louis's departure to elope to Fort Buford and join the Hunkpapas there.[6]

Legaré's train of carts reached Fort Buford on May 26 to witness an animated scene. Three steamboats, the *Far West*, the *Sherman*, and the *Helena*, were moored to the Fort Buford levee. The winter's ice had melted to open the Missouri for steamers, and the Indian prisoners could now be moved downriver. They were taking down their lodges and packing their provisions. Those in the warehouse were filing out to join those on the flats. Soldiers herded them aboard the three steamers. The vessels pushed off at five o'clock in the afternoon and turned down the Missouri River, headed for Standing Rock Agency, 290 miles distant. The Indians all went willingly, reported Major Brotherton, largely due to the efforts of Running Antelope, brought up from the agency because of his popularity. "His influence among his people is certainly wonderful," observed Brotherton.[7]

Those arriving with Jean Louis, including Many Horses and her suitor, were placed directly on one of the vessels. Far to the north, more than one hundred miles via Willow Bunch, Sitting Bull had reached Qu'Appelle on May 15. He had been told of his daughter's elopement and was said to be grieving deeply, an emotion that may have distracted him in his painful dealings with Indian Commissioner Dewdney at Qu'Appelle.[8]

In his two journeys Jean Louis had fed a total of fifty people, but the Indians had no other source of food, and the police and his own compassion had cast him in the role of persuading Sitting Bull and his followers to surrender at Fort Buford. Success would cost him mightily in provisions. Either the Indians would starve or he would have to assume responsibility for them until he could get them into the custody of the U.S. Army.

From the American standpoint, capturing Sitting Bull was vital. In the eyes of the American people he was still the butcher of the Little Bighorn, the slayer of General Custer. American newspapers had kept their readers advised of his whereabouts and the constant efforts of the Canadian police to persuade him to surrender. Each year his public image had grown. The diplomatic standoff in Washington, and the insult he had delivered to General Terry, reinforced and sustained the image. Americans wanted him neutralized. The press rarely mentioned other powerful Lakota chiefs, such as Four Horns and Black Moon. These chiefs and nearly all of the Lakotas still regarded Sitting Bull as the great chief that he was.

The effect of this constant and biased publicity on Sitting Bull was twofold. It enhanced his self-image, and it spawned lurid rumors of the treatment he could expect if he surrendered, which got back to him.

Sitting Bull and the people who had accompanied him to Qu'Appelle arrived back at Willow Bunch on July 2, 1881. There he learned that forty-eight of his people had gone with Jean Louis on his two trips to Buford and surrendered, including his eloping daughter. This news rocked Sitting Bull badly, causing him once more at least to think about giving up the resistance. The next morning, with all his chiefs and most of the warriors, Sitting Bull went to talk with Jean Louis and beg him to alleviate their acute hunger. "If you will give me what I want," he said, "I will do what you want me to do." In effect this was a promise to surrender, spurred by his anxiety over the fate of his daughter. But Jean Louis did not treat it as a matter of surrender. He knew the people were hungry, and he knew that food was what Sitting Bull would ask for first. Sitting Bull did, twelve sacks of flour. Jean Louis told them to come back in the afternoon, and he would give them all the provisions needed for a big feast, "whatever they wanted," and the twelve sacks of flour Sitting Bull had requested. In the afternoon all the chiefs and many of the people crowded into Jean Louis's store, and true to his word he laid out a big feast. The Indians ate all afternoon. At the conclusion of the feast Legaré announced that he had to leave for Buford soon. Sitting Bull said, "I am not ready. I want to stay here to have a rest." He still grasped at any excuse to delay the inevitable.

In response Jean Louis addressed Sitting Bull: "I have spent nearly all I have to feed you and can't wait any longer. I have to go to Buford soon with my carts. Anyone willing to come with me be ready in seven days." Also, those who intended to go with him should move away from the main camp and form a separate camp. No one replied.

Jean Louis then had twelve sacks of flour laid out on the floor. "They took the flour and departed," he noted. Either Sitting Bull had not yet made up his mind, or he was not ready to announce it.

At the end of seven days thirty-eight lodges, roughly two hundred adults and their children, had assembled a quarter of a mile from the store. Legaré began organizing them for departure, but the Indians asked for a delay. They had relatives at Wood Mountain they wanted to go with them. Jean Louis waited two days, then learned that only a few women remained at Wood Mountain, and they refused to leave.

On July 11 Jean Louis determined to begin the journey. He had hired eleven mixed-blood laborers for the mission, and at seven o'clock in the morning he had them bring out nearly all the provisions in his store and place them on the ground in front of Sitting Bull. Sitting Bull and the others grouped around him and simply stood there, saying nothing. After two hours Legaré declared that he had to get under way and asked if any were coming with him. Twenty lodges loaded their tipis and other possessions into twenty carts and got into line. But Sitting Bull, Four Horns, Black Moon, White Dog, and two other chiefs stopped their women from dismantling their lodges. Sitting Bull had resorted to his indecisive mode and taken other chiefs with him. Jean Louis left him to brood and got under way with twenty lodges, people and baggage packed into twenty carts. He left seventeen carts for the rest if they decided to come.

They did, but not to join Jean Louis's caravan. Sitting Bull had decided not to go to Fort Buford but, he told Jean Louis, to Milk River, and pointed his caravan to the west. What he imagined he would find there is puzzling. American troops were on the Missouri River downstream from the mouth of the Milk, as he surely knew from his own experience the previous winter. Perhaps he recalled the Milk River buffalo range. But at Milk River he could expect a much less generous welcome than Fort Buford offered.

Milk River remained the destination for only a short time. Jean Louis had made a temporary camp in midafternoon and shortly discovered the Sitting Bull caravan half a mile distant but not moving to join Legaré. He sent one of his laborers, Andre Gandre, to bring them in. Gandre found Sitting Bull and asked him where they were going. He pointed south, but a youth standing nearby said they were going west to Poplar River. Then all sat down, signifying that they were not joining Jean Louis's caravan. Gandre said if that if they were not going to the main party, Legaré wanted his outfit and provisions returned. As Gandre recalled, "The chief gave a grunt of dissent."

Jean Louis assembled his own carts and continued on the road to Buford, leaving Sitting Bull's party behind.

That night near midnight, with all bedded down, Sitting Bull and a throng of his men stormed into Jean Louis's camp. They were in a foul mood, waking sleeping people and prodding them to go back to Willow Bunch with them. They began rifling through John Louis's provisions, tormenting his horses, and piling sacks of flour on the backs of their horses. He stood quietly watching, but at daylight he protested their taking the flour. He saw one Indian piling sacks next to his horse and calling on others to come and get their share. Legaré went to him and ordered him to leave it alone. The Indian threw a sack on John Louis's foot and fired two rifle shots into it. After that episode Jean Louis feared for his life.

At midmorning on July 12 the caravan got under way, carrying Sitting Bull and all of his people. At the same time Jean Louis dispatched Andre Gandre and one of the Lakotas to take a letter to Major Brotherton. He wrote that he was on the way with Sitting Bull, Four Horns, Red Thunder, and four more chiefs, together with forty families, about two hundred men, women, and children. The messenger said they were about sixty miles out.[9]

The next morning, July 15, Brotherton replied to Jean Louis and dispatched six army wagons loaded with provisions to meet him. He sent a few soldiers to take care of the wagons but, as requested, no officer. He ordered the soldiers to report to Jean Louis so that he could direct the distribution of the rations. Brotherton had also sent a small present for each of the six chiefs. In presenting them, "You can say to them that I am told by the Department Commander to say to them all Sitting Bull included that they will be well treated here and they need fear nothing in coming in. Wagons will travel as fast as they can towards you. Shall be glad to see you when you get here."[10]

The wagons bearing food met Jean Louis's cavalcade fifty miles north of Buford on July 16. They contained seven sides of bacon, twenty bags of flour, and some coffee and sugar. The Indians paused long enough to stage a brief feast. The next day at noon an officer arrived from Fort Buford. Somehow, word had reached Brotherton that Sitting Bull might decide to break away from Jean Louis and head for another destination. Capt. Walter Clifford and five scouts rode for twelve hours, fifty-five miles, to reach the caravan. Clifford had been in charge of the prisoners held at Buford all winter and had a well-developed sympathy for the Indians. But he was determined that Sitting Bull would continue to Fort Buford.[11]

Clifford sought out Sitting Bull, who said "How," but nothing more. Sitting Bull then addressed his people, making one more attempt to avoid Fort Buford. He said, "We will go to Wolf Point, there we will cross the Missouri River and go into the Tongue River mountains. Once there we can hide and find game in abundance." More than five years had passed since the Lakotas had been in that country. Now, instead of game in abundance, it was filling up with stockmen and farmers. Besides, he and his people could never get there. They lacked the food and transportation and even stamina to travel very far before the soldiers caught them. If Sitting Bull was serious, he must have known such a scheme was impossible. His people knew it because he failed to persuade them.

That night, as the people were making their beds, an old woman stood and began to chant. It was a reassuring chant, in effect urging optimism rather than pessimism. Clifford's interpreter wrote it down for him:

> Be brave, my friends, be brave
> The white men have brought us food
> They will not hurt us
> My father and my mother, be not afraid
> Your hunger once more is stayed

And there is still food in abundance
My brother and my sister, comb your hair
And paint your faces with vermillion
For the Great Spirit has softened
The hearts of our enemies, and they feed us with food

Later that night Sitting Bull was in a better mood and decided to talk with Captain Clifford. Foremost in Sitting Bull's mind was his daughter, Many Horses. Someone had told him that she was being held in irons at Fort Yates. What had she done? What would happen to him? Clifford declared that this was not true. In fact "his daughter at Standing Rock was made quite a pet of instead of being in irons." Clifford had gained enough of Sitting Bull's confidence to relax him somewhat. Reflecting his continuing concern for his people, he asked about his friends at Standing Rock, especially Gall, Low Dog, Crow King, and Black Moon, "and when I told him how fat and jolly they were he laughed quite heartily." Jean Louis said this was the first time since crossing the line that Sitting Bull had been heard to talk or laugh. Clifford had indulged in some exaggeration about the people at Standing Rock, but they were being treated well, and above all they were not hungry.

The next morning, July 18, Captain Clifford dispatched a rider to Major Brotherton notifying him that the caravan would reach Fort Buford the next day. On July 19 all the inhabitants of the post gathered to watch the spectacle. Among them was a splash of scarlet. Captain Macdonell, sent by Colonel Irvine to report the surrender, had arrived the night before. The crowd of observers watched the caravan slowly approaching across the plain north of the fort.

Riding in advance, Sitting Bull and fourteen chiefs and headmen rode emaciated ponies. The group included two who for years had held an unshakable loyalty to Sitting Bull: Chief Four Horns and Sitting Bull's adopted nephew, One Bull. The other prominent chiefs had already surrendered. The ponies were followed by six army wagons and thirty-seven Red River carts belonging to Jean Louis. The wagons bore the women and children and the Red River carts the baggage and other possessions. Among the people on the wagons was Sitting Bull's family. They had stayed with him throughout the Canadian years and borne all the hardships of the rest of the Lakotas, including hunger. They consisted of his mother and two wives, two pairs of twins, an adolescent daughter, and two stepsons. The older sister, Many Horses, was at Standing Rock with her new husband.

At exactly noon, heralded by the loud screech of the ungreased wooden wheel hubs of the Red River carts, the caravan entered the fort and passed along the front of officers' row. Major Brotherton stood on his front porch with his adjutant, Lt. George S. Young, and Captain Macdonell, watching the procession pass by. Sitting Bull and Legaré rode in advance, but no one spoke or even acknowledged the others' presence.

The flat between the fort and the Missouri River had been designated for the Lakotas to camp. Brotherton had erected tipis for them. The major walked there to greet the arrivals. Sitting Bull dismounted and shook hands with Brotherton. The people unloaded the carts and established camp. Lieutenant Young gathered the small collection of firearms and took possession of the Indian ponies. Sitting Bull asked Major Brotherton if he could keep his prized Winchester and surrender it the next day.

A count revealed 44 men, 143 women, and their children. "They are some of them literally naked," Brotherton observed, "and with most of them the clothing is falling off of them from pure rotten-ness."[12] Sitting Bull was only slightly better clothed: a dirty calico shirt, black pants, and a dirty blanket loosely tied around his waist. He was afflicted with a severe eye infection and had tied a calico handkerchief around his head and drawn it partly across his eyes.

The surrender ceremony took place on July 20, 1881, in the parlor of Brotherton's quarters. Crowding the major's home were Major Brotherton, Captain Clifford, Captain Macdonell in his scarlet tunic, Capt. James Bell, Maj. Guido Ilges, an interpreter, and a St. Paul news-paperman, the only eyewitness correspondent to report the drama.[13] Attired in the same shabby clothing he had worn on arrival at the fort, Sitting Bull led thirty-two of his men in, and he was directed to sit in a chair with his rifle on the floor beneath him. On his right sat his six-year-old son, Crow Foot. Major Brotherton sat to his left.

Major Brotherton opened the session by explaining to Sitting Bull what the government planned to do with him and his people. They would be taken on a steamer down to Fort Yates and Standing Rock Agency, where kinsmen who had already surrendered were being settled. They would be well treated as long as they behaved themselves. The major then invited Sitting Bull to speak. The chief sat for five minutes saying nothing. Then he gestured to Crow Foot, who picked up the Winchester and handed it to Major Brotherton. Turning to the major, Sitting Bull said:

> I surrender this rifle to you through my young son, whom I now desire to teach in this manner that he has become a friend of the Americans. I wish him to learn the habits of the whites and to be educated as their sons are educated. I wish it to be remembered that I was the last man of my tribe to surrender my rifle. This boy has given it to you, and he now wants to know how he is going to make a living.

The last sovereign had yielded his and his people's sovereignty. It was a saddening experience, as his words suggest. Until his flight to Canada he had reigned over all five Lakota tribes, at least in name. His Hunkpapa tribe had remained solidly loyal for three decades. He had roamed free over the plains and mountains of his homeland. He treasured his freedom and never yielded any of it to the white man. As Crow Foot handed his father's rifle to the American officer, he marked the end of Lakota resistance, the end of Lakota freedom, and the end of the last Lakota sovereign.

Major Brotherton had told him what the government would do for him. Now he told the major what he expected from the government. He wanted all the Hunkpapas still at Willow Bunch, all those remaining at Poplar, and all those at Standing Rock, including his daughter, brought to join him and his followers at Fort Buford. Then he wanted a new reservation on the Little Missouri River set aside for the Hunkpapas. Beyond that,

> I now wish to be allowed to live on this side of the line or the other, as I see fit. I wish to continue my old life of hunting, but would like to trade on both sides of the line. This is my country, and I don't wish to be compelled to give it up. My heart was very sad at having to leave the Grandmother's country. She has been a friend to me, but I want my children to grow up in our native country, and I also wish to feel that I can visit two of my friends on the other side of the line—Major Walsh and Captain Macdonell—whenever I wish, and would like to trade with Louis Legaré, as he has always been a friend to me.

If Sitting Bull seriously believed that the government would honor his wishes, he was quickly disabused. Major Brotherton informed him that none of what he asked would be allowed. Sitting Bull argued that he had come in because his people were hungry and that the government had never given him anything. He believed he was entitled to some consideration. Brotherton said no. "All right, it is all of one piece. They have always lied to me."[14]

On July 29 the regular downriver steamer, ironically the *General Sherman*, docked at Fort Buford. Sitting Bull and his followers were led up the gangplank and settled on the deck. If Sitting Bull felt himself badly treated by the government, he was now to be welcomed by the white people who so recently had execrated him. On Sunday, July 31, the *Sherman* tied up at Bismarck. Citizens by the hundreds crowded the waterfront to get a glimpse of the famed chief they had so recently disparaged. The city fathers had arranged for Sitting Bull to see and experience some of the white man's ways.

The first was a railroad coach and locomotive. The Northern Pacific had built a spur line from the station to the riverside. The private car of the railway's general manager stood coupled to a locomotive. With Fish Allison interpreting, Sitting Bull was invited to board.

After carefully examining the coach he said he would rather walk. Instead Sitting Bull, his sister, Four Horns, and other chiefs crowded into a horse-drawn army ambulance and were driven up to the town. Citizens lined the road gawking at the chief. They noted that he was shabbily dressed in contrast to his comrades, who sported their best finery. In the old life such clothing had been a sign of generosity. He also wore a pair of smoked eyeglasses provided him at Fort Buford for his infected eyes.

At the Merchant's Hotel the group sat smoking and chatting with Fish Allison until summoned inside for a lavish banquet. Seated at a large table, Sitting Bull observed the way white people ate with forks, knives, and spoons, and did his best to emulate them. A bill of fare was provided to each of the diners. It listed all the courses to be served. As each arrived Fish Allison described what it was. Sitting Bull, so recently on the verge of starvation, now reveled in food he never knew existed. At the conclusion he told Fish Allison he did not understand how ice cream could be frozen in hot weather.

At the river dock he discovered another of the white man's customs. In Canada a trader had taught him how to write his name. The citizens paid money for his autograph and other items he was willing to part with. Back on the boat, he was wiser and richer than when he arrived.

The scene at Fort Yates was similarly uplifting. All his old friends welcomed him, and he had a tearful reunion with his daughter, Many Horses. He enjoyed long talks with Gall, Crow King, and others who had ridden with him in war and on the hunt. They and the other Hunkpapas were all settled in new homes at the adjacent Standing Rock Agency, but Sitting Bull and those who had surrendered with him waited impatiently for a decision. For three weeks they waited, until the post commander informed him that he and his people would be separated from the rest of the Hunkpapas and taken farther down the river, to Fort Randall, where they would be held as prisoners of war. Infantry with fixed bayonets forced them aboard a steamer. One Bull resisted and was struck in the back with a rifle butt.

Again the government had lied to Sitting Bull. He had been told that he and those who had surrendered with him would live at Standing Rock. Now they would live far down the river as prisoners of war.

For all the exposure to white ways at Bismarck, Sitting Bull had not changed his mind about his steadfast resistance and the life he was now about to live:

White men like to dig in the ground for their food. My people prefer to hunt the buffalo as their fathers did. White men like to stay in one place. My people want to move their tepees here and there to different hunting grounds. The life of white men is slavery. They are prisoners in towns or farms. The life my people want is a life of freedom. I have seen nothing that a white man has, houses or railways or clothing or food, that is as good as the right to move in the open country, and live in our own fashion.[15]

It was not to be.

Epilogue

On September 17, 1881, the steamer *Sherman* docked at Fort Randall, Dakota, three hundred miles down the Missouri River from Standing Rock Agency. Sitting Bull and the following that had surrendered with him filed down the gangplank under the guard of a contingent of black soldiers. The secretary of war had ruled that these people be held as prisoners of war. How they differed from the Hunkpapas who had already surrendered and were now settled at Standing Rock Agency was not explained. Sitting Bull went to the commanding officer, Col. George S. Andrews, and asked why he was sent here and how long he would have to stay. Although sympathetic to the Indians, Colonel Andrews could not answer because he did not know.

As directed by their guards, the people raised thirty-two tipis half a mile west of the river. On all sides the soldiers kept watch. Rationed by the army, the prisoners had nothing to do but sit, eat, ruminate about their confinement, and visit with friends.

However, in December 1881 Sitting Bull found a task that kept him busy. The Rev. John P. Williamson, missionary at the Yankton agency across the Missouri River, appeared with a sheaf of copies of pictographs Sitting Bull had drawn years before. They had made their way through official circles and to Sitting Bull for his comment. These reminders of the past aroused his interest in producing more, especially as gifts for local army officers and traders who had done him favors. During 1882 he drew at least three groups of pictographs, tailored for a white audience rather than depicting feats of war against the whites.[1]

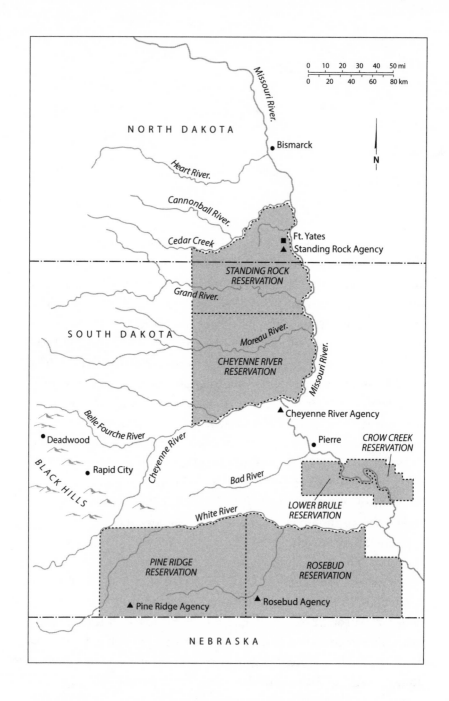

Map 3. The Sioux Reservations in 1890. Bill Nelson Cartography.

But the why and the how long remained distressing questions, and the people grew increasingly restive. Paradoxically, an Indian solved half the problem—the how long. Strike the Ree, chief of the Yankton Sioux, persuaded Reverend Williamson to help him draft a letter to Secretary of War Robert T. Lincoln urging Sitting Bull's release from prisoner-of-war status. Strike the Ree's powerful words moved the secretary, who forwarded the letter to Secretary of the Interior Henry M. Teller with his own endorsement of the plea.

Strike the Ree's noble gesture worked. Sitting Bull and his people were no longer prisoners of war but agency Indians. On May 10, 1883, the steamboat *Behan* docked at Fort Yates, and they filed down the gangway to take up residence at Standing Rock. Sitting Bull had often declared that he did not want an agent over him. Now he had one. James McLaughlin would reign over Sitting Bull for the rest of his life.

It was a daunting task for McLaughlin because Sitting Bull regarded himself as the head chief, as he had always been. He would cooperate with McLaughlin, but he would expect him to yield on all matters of disagreement. The day after landing, Sitting Bull marched into McLaughlin's office and presented his first demands. He expected the rations and other issue goods to be turned over to him to distribute among his people as he saw fit. Moreover, he had appointed eleven chiefs and thirteen headmen and wanted them confirmed by the agent. McLaughlin labeled the demands "inflated nonsense" and informed Sitting Bull that he would be treated like any other Indian at Standing Rock. As Sitting Bull was to learn, McLaughlin prevailed in any dispute because he controlled the rations, the Indian police, and the Indian courts, and he knew how to use them.

McLaughlin was an experienced agent, valued by the government, by the hundreds of Indian rights activists back East, and by the Roman Catholic Church. Unlike the many incompetent and corrupt Indian agents of that time, McLaughlin managed his agency honestly and with firm authority.[2]

Sitting Bull and McLaughlin formed an instant dislike for each other. They clashed repeatedly over both major and minor issues, most having to do with agency regulations. Part of the hostility between the two lay in the fact that Sitting Bull still regarded himself as the supreme chief, and the loyalty of most of the reservation Indians reinforced his claim. Moreover, while Sitting Bull never yielded his faith in the old ways of freedom, he made a modest effort to learn and practice some of the ways of the white man. The first season he reluctantly heeded the command of McLaughlin to plant a garden.

Sitting Bull arrived at Standing Rock just as the government's "civilization" program was getting under way. The tools in that program were schools that taught the white man's way, churches that promoted Christianity, Indian police to enforce the white man's law, and Indian courts. The Courts of Indian Offenses, with Indian judges, tried not only the usual misdemeanors and felonies but also a List of Indian Offenses. "Heathenish dances" such as the Sun Dance, war dance, and scalp dance; plural marriage; and the practices of medicine men were among the Indian offenses.

Sitting Bull felt his influence waning as McLaughlin cultivated Lakota rivals and sought to break up tribal institutions. Running Antelope and Crow King died, and McLaughlin's favors set up Gall as a rival of Sitting Bull. Gall proved pliable and tried to shove Sitting Bull into the background. Gall's manipulation had an effect. Sitting Bull rarely appeared in public, but when he did his people showed that they had not forgotten him and the years of freedom in which he had led them. He and the most loyal Hunkpapas erected their log cabins on Grand River, thirty-five miles south of the agency and comfortably distant from the hostile agent.

Not only were the reservations in the grip of the civilization program, but both government and settlers wanted Lakota land. The Great Sioux Reservation, all of the present state of South Dakota west of the Missouri River, embraced 120 million acres of land. Break up the Great Sioux Reservation into six separate reservations, one for each of the Lakota tribes, ran the argument. This would leave half the reservation, about sixty million acres, to open to white settlement. Complicating the measure for the government was the treaty requirement that any cession of land had to be approved by a vote of three-fourths of the adult Lakota males. That set off years of contention as the government held votes at each of the agencies. It also sowed factions within each tribe and disrupted tribal cohesion.

For Sitting Bull, the issue first arose three months after his arrival from Fort Randall. A special Senate committee chaired by Sen. Henry L. Dawes, a devoted friend of the Indian, visited Standing Rock in August 1883. Their purpose was to learn the Indians' views of the land proposal. The committee and the leading chiefs spoke in generalities, although Sitting Bull remained silent. When Senator Dawes asked him if he had anything to say, he rose and asked, "Do you know who I am?" He repeated the question several times, then proclaimed, "I want to tell you that if the Great Spirit has chosen anyone to be the chief of this country it is myself." He then dared to upbraid the senators: "You have conducted yourselves like men who have been drinking whiskey, and I came here to give you some advice." He then waved his hand, and all the Indians in the room rose and left. Gall's schemes may have undermined Sitting Bull, but they had not seriously curtailed his powerful influence with the people.

At a later session Sitting Bull apologized to the senators for his words, but then launched into another diatribe. "I have always been a chief, and have been made chief of all the land." A rambling speech followed. It was too much for John A. Logan, a powerful senator who had been a general in the Civil War. "You were not appointed by the Great Spirit," he roared. "Appointments are not made that way. If it were not for the government, you would be freezing and starving today in the mountains." If he ever acted like this again, "you will be put in the guard-house, and be made to work." Shamed in front of fellow tribesmen, Sitting Bull stole out of the room.[3]

He did act like this again, as the land issue exploded after the Dawes Act of 1887. It provided for an allotment of 160 acres to each household on the reservation and, after all on a reservation had been enrolled, sale of the surplus land to the government. It would then be opened to white settlement under the Homestead Act of 1862. But the Dakota land champions refused to wait that long. They pushed through Congress a law reversing the sequence so that the "surplus" land would be obtained before surveys had been run, Indians had been registered, and allotments had been made—in other words, immediately.

Sitting Bull fought hard against this new law. He constantly asserted that there was no such thing as surplus land. There was not enough now for their children and grandchildren. The law was a scheme of the white man to get as much as possible of the Lakotas' land and to get it now. Although the tribes all opposed yielding any of their land, they were manipulated by government agents, divided into factions, and warned of severe consequences if they voted no, But after the votes were counted, the white man got sixty million acres of the Lakotas' land and the Great Sioux Reservation no longer existed—an even worse outcome than Sitting Bull had foretold.

While Sitting Bull battled the theft of Indian land throughout the 1880s, he and his family, residing in two log cabins on Grand River, worked at farming. A district farmer employed by the agency taught them the rudiments of farming, and they prospered. According to One Bull, in the years after 1884 Sitting Bull's agricultural pursuits rewarded him with twenty horses, forty-five cows, eighty chickens, and fields of oats, corn, and potatoes. This was a remarkable achievement for one who had vowed never to plant the soil.[4]

Living with him at Grand River were his two wives and five children, one of whom was Crow Foot, his adolescent son, who was so smart that people said he had grown up too fast. Testifying to Sitting Bull's fecundity, one child had been born in 1887 and another in 1888. His beloved mother, who had lived in his lodge for twenty-four years, died in 1884. She had served as a tower of strength for her son and never hesitated to give him advice. Above all, year after year she urged him to stay out of battle. He had always relied on her, and her loss was an occasion for deep mourning.

With all his devotion to the old ways, Sitting Bull was curious about the white ways, his appetite whetted by the lavish banquet in the Bismarck hotel on the way down from Fort Buford. In September 1883 he headed the Indian delegation to the ceremony laying the cornerstone of the new territorial capitol building in Bismarck. He sat with the celebrities, was introduced from the platform, and rode in a parade that included former president Grant, two interior secretaries, and other dignitaries. They were on their way to Montana to drive the last spike in the Northern Pacific Railway.

Thinking that such outside visits might push Sitting Bull down the road to civilization, McLaughlin took him on an official trip to St. Paul in March 1884. The Northern Pacific provided passes for the journey. Sitting Bull took one of his wives and One Bull. McLaughlin's wife, a Dakota Sioux Indian, went as interpreter. In St. Paul they put up in a hotel, a new experience for Sitting Bull, and set forth on a tour of businesses, industrial plants, the *St. Paul Pioneer Press*, and school classrooms, all of which not only entertained Sitting Bull but astonished him too. The climax came at a fire station, where the firefighters staged a demonstration. The bell clanged; the men slid down a pole, harnessed the horses and hooked them to the engines, and dashed away. Sitting Bull was so enthralled that he demanded an encore. This time he set off the alarm himself.

Sitting Bull discovered that he was a celebrity in the outside world. He sold enough autographs to return home with a tidy sum. At each stop on the return journey from St. Paul, he descended to the platform and put himself on exhibit. Showmen also discovered that Sitting Bull was a celebrity and sought permission to take him on tour. The one who prevailed was William F. Cody, "Buffalo Bill," who obtained official permission to enlist Sitting Bull as a feature of his famed "Wild West." The show toured the country for four months in the summer of 1885. Cody did not sensationalize Sitting Bull but had him ride in the parade, then sit in front of a tipi, greet visitors, and sell his autograph. McLaughlin later criticized him for giving away his money to "street urchins." In Washington DC, Cody took Sitting Bull to the Executive Mansion to leave a letter for Pres. Grover Cleveland, then next door to the War Department to meet Gen. Philip H. Sheridan, now commanding the army. The Indian delegation showed great interest in the paintings of western scenes on the wall but studiously ignored the fat little general in the blue coat.[5]

The season ended in St. Louis in October. In the lobby of the Southern Hotel he sat with Col. Eugene A. Carr, and the two reminisced about fighting each other on the plains only a decade before. He also told a reporter he liked show business but was tired and wanted to go back to the fresh air of the prairies.

Throughout the tour Sitting Bull had ridden a light gray horse of which he became fond. Cody presented it to him and paid to have it shipped to Standing Rock. It remained Sitting Bull's favorite horse for the rest of his life.

Sitting Bull made no more tours. McLaughlin changed his mind about their benefits. Sitting Bull had returned "vain and obstinate" and had squandered his earnings. "For the good of the service" McLaughlin opposed any more tours.

By 1889 the Lakotas on all the six reservations had fallen into despair. The land agreements had cost them half of the Great Sioux Reservation, sixty million acres. Scorching dry winds had killed their crops, and Congress had delayed appropriations for so long that their rations had to be severely cut. Sickness swept the reservations. And the government had made progress in breaking down the old life and substituting the new, dividing the people into feuding "progressives" and "nonprogressives."

In summer 1889 a rumor swept all the reservations in the West that far to the west a Messiah had appeared to rescue the Indians from their adversities. It proved a story so compelling that a delegation from Rosebud, Pine Ridge, and Cheyenne River reservations journeyed west to try to find this savior. They found him in Nevada: a Paiute holy man named Wovoka. He told the Lakotas of a new religion, the Ghost Dance. By dancing a prescribed dance, they could bring about a new world, teeming with game, devoid of whites, and peopled by their ancestors.

The Lakota delegates, led by a Miniconjou named Kicking Bear, returned in spring 1890. Kicking Bear emerged as the apostle of the new religion, and his inspiring words found many converts in the Pine Ridge and Rosebud reservations south of Standing Rock. As the summer wore away with the same calamities as the previous summer, Sitting Bull sent a party to invite Kicking Bear to visit Standing Rock. On October 13, 1890, at Sitting Bull's settlement on Grand

River, Kicking Bear preached a powerful sermon, so powerful that One Bull, now an officer in the agency police force, the *ceska maza*, hastened to the agency and repeated it for McLaughlin. The agent sent police captain Crazy Walking and a squad of policemen, including One Bull, to drive Kicking Bear and his acolytes off the Standing Rock Reservation. But Crazy Walking, intimidated by Kicking Bear, merely ordered him to leave. Sitting Bull promised that he would leave the next day. McLaughlin sent Lieutenant Chatka and another policeman to make sure Kicking Bear had left. He had not, so Chatka escorted him and his protégés to the reservation boundary.

Kicking Bear had accomplished his mission, planting the Ghost Dance at Standing Rock. Sitting Bull's log village became the setting for daily Ghost Dances, as the people moved from their scattered homes to set up camps and dance. On the outskirts of the Grand River village they erected a row of sweat lodges, a prayer tree, and a dance circle. Those who danced with sufficient intensity fell to the ground in a trance and visited the promised land and their ancestors. Sitting Bull did not dance, but he raised a tipi next to the dance circle and encouraged all who came to dance. He seems to have alternated between belief and nonbelief, according to the local missionary, but he acted as Standing Rock's apostle for it. The role, carried out daily, heightened his power.

One Bull was no longer in the embarrassing position of opposing his uncle and adopted father. Captain Bull Head had told McLaughlin that One Bull had embraced the new religion, which he had not, and he was dismissed from the police force.

As winter 1890–91 approached, turmoil swept all the Lakota reservations. Kicking Bear had enjoined the people to dance all winter so that the new world would come in the spring. The word also spread that the dance would make the bullets of the white man's guns fall to the ground. The dancers danced and badly frightened the white settlers surrounding the reservations. All the agents except McLaughlin feared violence, but the agent at Pine Ridge, Daniel F. Royer, was especially scared by "these crazy dancers." Repeatedly he called for troops to protect the agency personnel.[6]

That happened on November 20, 1890. Troops occupied Pine Ridge and Rosebud agencies. McLaughlin and all the agents were notified that in matters relating to the Indian troubles, they were to act under the direction of the army's local post commander. For McLaughlin, that was the Fort Yates commander, Lt. Col. William F. Drum. They got along well and agreed on the best measures for handling the Ghost Dance. So did Drum's department commander in St. Paul, Brig. Gen. Thomas H. Ruger. But superior to both was the division commander in Chicago, Maj. Gen. Nelson A. Miles. The Lakotas had once called him Bear Coat. He had risen to high rank and had not lost any of his disdain for Indians.

McLaughlin and the other agents had received orders to remove "leaders of disaffection" from the reservations and imprison them elsewhere until the storm abated. For McLaughlin, this offered the means of getting rid of Sitting Bull. He wanted to use his Indian police to arrest him, not soldiers, and Colonel Drum backed him. Not until winter set in and sent the dancers to their cabins did McLaughlin intend to move, but winter was late setting in.

On November 28 a strange group of men arrived at Fort Yates: Buffalo Bill Cody and some of his staff. He bore orders from General Miles directing him to secure the person of Sitting Bull and deliver him to the nearest commander of U.S. troops. He also presented Miles's calling card, handed to him at a banquet in Chicago, on which were written orders for commanders of troops to aid Cody in any way requested.

Both McLaughlin and Drum were chagrined. At best Cody would renew an old friendship but fail to talk Sitting Bull into submitting to arrest; at worst, Cody might get himself killed by dancers. But Cody and his men could not undertake this mission immediately because he was "somewhat intoxicated." Colonel Drum's officers conspired to keep him that way all night in the Fort Yates officers' club. The next morning, however, he emerged ready to ride the thirty-five miles to Grand River. Halfway to his destination, he was informed by one of McLaughlin's Grand River spies that Sitting Bull was already on his way to the agency on a parallel road. Cody returned to the agency only to find that some quick use of the telegraph by McLaughlin had brought a presidential order canceling the mission. Cody returned to Chicago to bill the army for his expenses and to make Miles angry at Ruger and Drum.

On December 12 Colonel Drum received a dispatch from General Ruger: General Miles had instructed him to order Drum to arrest Sitting Bull at once. Drum consulted with McLaughlin, and they agreed that the arrest had to be made and would be made on the next ration day, December 20, by the Indian police contingent at Grand River under Capt. Bull Head. Drum's soldiers would hide behind the hills in case they were needed.

This timetable was disrupted when one of Sitting Bull's comrades, Bull Ghost, brought word to McLaughlin that Sitting Bull wanted a pass to leave the reservation. When troops had occupied Pine Ridge and Rosebud, the dance leaders and their acolytes had taken positions on an elevation known as the Stronghold. Now they had invited Sitting Bull to visit them there. He believed he ought to go.

This word reached McLaughlin on December 12, the same day Colonel Drum received his orders to arrest Sitting Bull. The two made plans to seize Sitting Bull as soon as possible. Two days of exchanging messages between McLaughlin and his Grand River allies set the date at December 15. Captain Bull Head would lead his police from his cabin down Grand River and enter the village. Drum would send two troops of cavalry to lie in concealment and charge in if needed. Sitting Bull owned two cabins. On this night he slept in one with one of his wives, a child, and Crow Foot, now fourteen years old. Others crowded the cabin, having taken refuge there after the dance. The rest of his family were in the other cabin.

At six o'clock, the morning dark, drizzly, and cold, the police struck. Sergeant Shave Head kicked in the door and seized Sitting Bull as other police crowded into the room. The sergeant said, "Brother, we came after you." "How, all right," replied Sitting Bull, who submitted quietly. But he remonstrated with them for not letting him dress. He had to send to the other cabin for the clothes he wanted to wear. That took time. Barking dogs had aroused the villagers, all of whom were Sitting Bull's followers. A mob converged on the cabin. As earlier instructed, one of the police had brought Sitting Bull's gray circus horse from the corral and saddled it for departure.

Emerging from the cabin, Bull Head grasped one of Sitting Bull's arms and Shave Head the other. Sergeant Red Tomahawk stood behind him with a pistol in his hand. A squad of frightened policemen lined the front of the cabin, trying to keep the howling crowd at bay. Catch the Bear, long a bitter enemy of Bull Head's, shouted, "Now here are the ceska maza, just as we expected all the time. You think you are going to take him. You shall not do it." As armed men pushed to the front of the crowd, Crow Foot spoke up, "Well, you always called yourself a brave chief. Now you are allowing yourself to be taken by the ceska maza." After a few moments Sitting Bull replied, "Then I shall not go." He hung back as police implored him not to resist.

Amid the turmoil, Catch the Bear raised his Winchester and fired. The bullet hit Bull Head in his right side. As he fell, he turned his pistol on Sitting Bull and shot him in the chest. From behind, Red Tomahawk shot him in the back of his head. Catch the Bear fired again, striking Shave Head in the stomach. All four fell into a heap. Another policeman jumped on Catch the Bear, grabbed his rifle, clubbed and then shot him. Inside the cabin the police killed Crow Foot.

The fight went on, with more casualties, until the soldiers intervened.

A vision had alerted Sitting Bull that he would die at the hands of his own people. Two bullets fired by blue-clad members of his own tribe had validated the prophecy and ended the life of the greatest chief of the Lakotas, the greatest chief of any of the western Indian tribes.[7]

In Winnipeg, Manitoba, James M. Walsh read the local newspaper on December 16. He placed on his desk a sheet of paper with the letterhead of Dominion Coal, Coke, and Transportation Company, and penned a paragraph:

I am glad to learn that Bull is relieved of his miseries even if it took the bullet to do it. A man who wields so much power as Bull once did, that of a King, over a wild spirited people cannot endure abject poverty slavery and beggary without suffering great mental pain and death is a relief. . . . Bull's confidence and belief in the Great Spirit was stronger than I ever saw in any other man. He trusted him implicitly. . . . History does not tell us that a greater Indian than Bull ever lived, he was the Mohommat of his people the law and king maker of the Sioux.

Sitting Bull's adherents fought a battle with Colonel Drum's cavalry and escaped to the south. There, on December 29, the conflict reached its nadir with the tragedy at Wounded Knee on the Pine Ridge Reservation. Without further bloodshed, Major General Miles directed the roundup of the scattered bands and returned them to their homes. The Ghost Dance had failed to deliver the promised land.

More than any person, Jean Louis Legaré was responsible for the surrender of Sitting Bull. E. H. "Fish" Allison came close, but the rash military actions of Maj. Guido Ilges at the Poplar Agency caused Sitting Bull to turn back to Canada. In the absence of Major Walsh, only Jean Louis had the resources, the compassion, and the determination to draw Sitting Bull into Fort Buford.

Acting on these motives, Jean Louis had nearly bankrupted himself by providing provisions for Sitting Bull and his people to eat while still at Willow Bunch and on the journey to Fort Buford. He devoted nearly full time to the enterprise, thus forgoing profits from his trading post. In the final run to Fort Buford he almost got himself killed by the Indians, and he completed the journey in a state of high anxiety.

After some initial skepticism, Major Brotherton came to appreciate the work Jean Louis was doing and repeatedly told him that the government would almost certainly provide him compensation. He lacked the authority to negotiate a contract, however, so Jean Louis had to content himself with Brotherton's verbal assurances. The major did appeal to department headquarters on August 30, 1881, but nothing came of it. When Jean Louis himself submitted a claim in May 1882, Brotherton proved of no help: "I consider this whole thing an afterthought, and something which Mr. Legare has been induced to get up, or which has been gotten up for him, by interested parties."

The years rolled by with no sign of compensation and no sign of any further effort to secure it. Brotherton, whose army record was undistinguished, moved on to other assignments. After waiting seven years for some indication of recompense, Jean Louis sued the United States.[8] His deposition is rich in the history of his achievement, and others contributed significantly, especially Andre Gandre and the police captain Alexander Macdonell. Legaré claimed $13,412 for provisions, which he itemized. The court allowed this amount, but bureaucratic fumbling delayed the payment until 1905, when he received only $5,000. In the meantime he had petitioned the Canadian government for $5,000, which allowed him $2,000.

Jean Louis lived a vigorous and productive life after the Sitting Bull episode. A community of Métis lived at Willow Bunch and were often in the same starving condition as the Lakotas had been. Jean Louis helped them frequently.

When Louis Riel led the Métis Rebellion of 1885, the Willow Bunch Métis preferred to take no part in the uprising. They were starving, however, and Jean Louis gained them employment by persuading the authorities to let him recruit a unit of Métis scouts to aid the North-West Mounted Police in patrolling the area of conflict. They performed satisfactorily for two months, but the police preferred their own leadership to Legaré's, and he returned to Willow Bunch.

As one of the founders of Willow Bunch, Jean Louis took an active part in community affairs. He held the offices of justice of the peace, census enumerator, postmaster, and school trustee. A devout Roman Catholic, in 1906 he donated eighty acres to his parish for a new church and rectory. He also assisted the local clergy in the settlement of French-Canadians, who by the early 1900s had displaced the Métis as the majority group in Willow Bunch.

Shortly after the surrender of Sitting Bull, Jean Louis established a cattle ranch at Willow Bunch and later a horse ranch. He kept his herds at seven hundred cattle and one thousand horses. Ranching proved more profitable than his effort to establish a cheese factory, which failed. His hotel and restaurant thrived (he was said to give away more food to the starving than he gained in profits).

Jean Louis and the wife he had married before establishing himself at Wood Mountain in 1873 led a productive and influential life at Willow Bunch. Throughout he was noted for his modesty and humility. Apart from his role in the surrender of Sitting Bull, Willow Bunch is a part of his legacy. In 1960 it established a regional park in his honor, and the national government erected a plaque to commemorate his life.

Jean Louis Legaré died in Willow Bunch on February 1, 1918, at age seventy-six.

His claim for compensation in bringing Sitting Bull to Fort Buford did not die with him. It was brought to vigorous life by his great-grandson, Edward Albert Legaré, who lived at Regina, Saskatchewan. He researched the issue, wrote papers, gave speeches, stirred newspaper publicity, and sought ways to reactivate the official claim. As late as 1996, he asked the advice of the present author. I advised him to seek the aid of the North Dakota congressional delegation. Sen. Byron Dorgan inquired of the Justice Department and predictably discovered that nothing more could be done.

Canadian Jean Louis Legaré played an important role in American history. He was unjustly treated by the American government, and he is hardly remembered today.

Maj. James M. Walsh played no role in the surrender of Sitting Bull. In 1880, a year earlier, Walsh had been exiled to his home in Brockville, Ontario, by Premier Sir John A. Macdonald. Walsh was suspected not only of failing to press Sitting Bull hard enough to surrender, but later of working to prevent his surrender. Ironically, earlier Walsh had had strong political connections in the Conservative government of Macdonald, which led to his appointment to high rank when the

North-West Mounted Police was formed in 1873. Walsh alone could have induced Sitting Bull to surrender, but Macdonald kept him on leave in Brockville until after Jean Louis Legaré had led Sitting Bull and his following onto the Fort Buford parade ground.

Although Walsh had dealt with Sitting Bull exceptionally well, he had antagonized many officers of the North-West Mounted Police. They disliked his flamboyant ways, his constant favorable newspaper publicity, and his close friendship with the Lakotas. As he reveled in the sobriquet "Sitting Bull's boss," some in the force resented it. It was also rumored that he had fathered a child with a Blackfeet woman and maintained sexual relations with Lakota women.

Walsh was bitter over his treatment by the Macdonald government in separating him from Sitting Bull, but remained in the police until forced to resign in 1883.

Walsh's life after the Mounted Police was not especially distinguished. With the Canadian Pacific Railway building westward, he settled in Winnipeg, Manitoba, and became manager of the Dominion Coal, Coke and Transportation Company, which exploited the Souris coalfields.'

Earlier in his life Walsh's politics had rested with the Conservatives, which accounted for his high rank in the North-West Mounted Police. After his shabby treatment by the Conservatives, however, he drifted toward the Liberals. He became a close friend of the rising Liberal politician Clifford Sifton. When the Liberals won the premiership in 1896, Walsh achieved a measure of renown, if not revenge, by writing Prime Minister Wilfrid Laurier a long letter explaining why the North-West Mounted Police should be greatly reduced, if not abolished altogether.

Sifton became minister of the interior in the Laurier government and rewarded Walsh. By the summer of 1897 the Klondike gold rush was well under way. The Mounted Police were brought in to police the Yukon Territory. In August 1897 Walsh was named commissioner of the Yukon Territory and reinstated as a superintendent in the Mounted Police, then in October he was given command of all the Mounted Police in the territory. Under instructions from Sifton,

Walsh communicated directly with Ottawa, bypassing police head-quarters in Regina and making Walsh's Yukon contingent virtually an independent police force.

If Walsh had friends in the Mounted Police, he lost most of them in the Yukon. His high command angered the entire force. But Walsh proved an inept administrator as Yukon commissioner, and he resigned in the spring of 1898, completing less than one year, and went home to Brockville.

He died of a heart attack in Brockville on July 25, 1905, at the age of sixty-five.

James Morrow Walsh's legacy is confined mainly to the three years he dealt with Sitting Bull, 1877–80. Rather than "Sitting Bull's Boss," it might be labeled "The Story of a Friendship."

Throughout Sitting Bull's life, including his years in Canada, no one was closer to him than One Bull, his nephew and adopted son. He performed any task, pleasant or disagreeable, easy or difficult, that Sitting Bull might wish. In Canada, when Sitting Bull's policy was to prevent any of his followers from returning to their homeland, One Bull was chief of the akicita, the village police.

One Bull was not in Sitting Bull's cabin on the day he died, although his other wife slept in the second cabin. Rather, One Bull was hauling freight from the railroad down to Standing Rock. What his actions might have been had he been present when the ceska maza burst into Sitting Bull's cabin is speculative.

One Bull spent the rest of his life on the Standing Rock Reservation. He was thirty-seven in 1890, and he lived a long and contented life until his death, at age ninety-four, in 1947. In 1928 he met Walter Stanley Campbell, a University of Oklahoma professor who wrote under the pen name of Stanley Vestal. He was researching a biography of Sitting Bull. At seventy-five One Bull's memory of his life with Sitting Bull was still sharp. Other Hunkpapa and Miniconjou old men also remembered the years of their youth, when they battled other tribesmen and the white people. They gloried in the memory of those years and often reminisced about them among themselves.

Some consented to let Vestal tell their story. The result is not only books by Vestal but, even more important to the historian, the vast collection of his papers in the University of Oklahoma Library Western History Collections. None are more valuable for glimpsing Sitting Bull than Vestal's interviews with One Bull.

That is the legacy of One Bull, known at Standing Rock as Chief Henry Oscar One Bull.

Notes

ABBREVIATIONS

AAAG   Acting Assistant Adjutant General
AAG   Assistant Adjutant General
AGO   Adjutant General's Office
AGUSA   Adjutant General, U.S. Army
AR   Annual Report
CO   Commanding Officer
MS   Manuscript
NAC   National Archives of Canada
NARA   National Archives and Records Administration
RG   Record Group
SW   Secretary of War
NWMP   North-West Mounted Police
LR   Letters Received
OAG   Office of Adjutant General
DD   Department of Dakota
MDM   Military Division of the Missouri

1. SITTING BULL

1. In most treatments of the life of Sitting Bull, this episode is either ignored or controversial. My account is based entirely on Indian sources, gathered in the collection of Walter S. Campbell (Stanley Vestal) in the Western History Collections of the University of Oklahoma Library (hereafter cited as the Campbell Collection). They are interviews Campbell conducted in the late 1920s and early 1930s with Lakota Indians who were contemporaries of Sitting Bull. The head

chief ceremony is drawn from Robert P. Higheagle Manuscript, box 104, folder 21, pp. 2, 43; Higheagle, "Twenty-five Songs Made by Sitting Bull," box 104, folder 17; One Bull, box 104; One Bull folder, no. 11, MS 127; White Bull, "Life of Sitting Bull," box 105, notebook 4; White Bull, notebook 8; White Bull, box 106, notebook 53; Old Bull, box 105, notebook 11. White Bull was present at this ceremony.

2. I formed my estimate of Sitting Bull in researching and writing his biography: Utley, *Lance and the Shield*.

3. One Bull, "Why Sitting Bull Wears a White Eagle Feather as a Head Ornament," box 104, folder 20; and Robert P. Higheagle MS, box 104, folder 21, p. 46. Both in Campbell Collection. Stanley Vestal relied on his interviews to write two books: *Sitting Bull: Champion of the Lakotas* (New York: Houghton Mifflin, 1932) (the latest printing is Norman: University of Oklahoma Press, 1969); *Warpath: The True Story of the Fighting Sioux, Told in a Biography of Chief White Bull* (Lincoln: University of Nebraska Press, 1984) (the first edition was published in 1934). As I have written elsewhere, Campbell's specialty was creative writing, which characterizes both books. They contain useful information if one has been through the interviews themselves. Otherwise, their reliability is suspect.

4. One Bull, "Why Sitting Bull Wears a Red Feather as a Head Ornament," MS, box 104, folder 20, Campbell Collection.

5. One Bull, MS 127, box 104, folder 11, Campbell Collection.

6. One Bull, box 105, notebook 12; Robert P. Higheagle MS, box 4, folder 21, pp. 17–18, Campbell Collection.

7. One Bull, box 104, folder 6. White Bull, box 105, notebook 8, Campbell Collection.

8. Higheagle, "Twenty-five Songs Made by Sitting Bull," MS, box 104, folder 17, Campbell Collection. See also Two Bulls, "Sitting Bull's Kindness to Birds," MS, box 104, folder 20, Campbell Collection.

9. Clow, "Mad Bear," 132–49. Utley, *Frontiersmen in Blue*, 113–20.

10. Larpenteur, *Forty Years a Fur Trader*, 358–60.

11. Marquis, *Warrior Who Fought Custer*, 205.

12. White Bull, box 105, notebook 23; White Bull folder, no.12; Old Bull, box 105, notebooks 1, 2, and 9; and box 106, notebook 51, Campbell Collection.

13. Old Bull, box 106, notebook 51, Campbell Collection. Robertson, "We Are Going to Have a Big Lakota War," 2–15.

14. Custer to AAAG Yellowstone Expedition, Pompey's Pillar, August 15, 1873, RG 393, Division of the Missouri Special Files, M1495, roll 1, frame 719ff., NARA. White Bull, box 105, notebook 24, Campbell Collection.

15. Marquis, *Warrior Who Fought Custer*, 178–79.

16. White Bull, box 105, notebook 8; One Bull, box 104, folder 10, and box 105, notebook 19. Both Campbell Collection.

17. One Bull and White Bull, box 104, folder 6; box 105, notebook 24, p. 48. Both Campbell Collection.

18. DeMallie, *The Sixth Grandfather*, 181, 184, 190.

19. Moving Robe Woman, interview with Frank B. Zahn, 1931, in Hardoff, *Lakota Recollections*, 93.

20. Campbell interview with White Bull, box 105, notebook 24, Campbell Collection. I treat the Battle of the Little Bighorn in my biography of Sitting Bull and my biography of Custer: *Lance and the Shield* and *Cavalier in Buckskin*.

21. Campbell interview with One Bull, box 105, notebook 19, Campbell Collection. Mary C. Collins interview with One Bull, box 2, folder 34, Collins Papers, South Dakota Historical Society.

22. Graham, *The Custer Myth*, 60.

23. Campbell interview with One Bull, box 105, notebooks 19 and 41, Campbell Collection. Campbell interview with Gray Whirlwind, box 105, notebook 14, Campbell Collection.

24. One Bull, box 105, notebook 11, Campbell Collection.

25. Lt. Col. Elwell S. Otis to AAG Department of Dakota, Glendive, Oct. 27, 1876, in SW, *Annual Report* (1876), 515–18. Gray, "Peace-Talkers" and "Sitting Bull Strikes." *Army and Navy Journal* 14 (February 10, 1877): 431.

26. Gray, "Peace-Talkers," 18. For the events that followed, see Greene, *Yellowstone Command*, chap. 5. Campbell interview with White Bull, box 105, notebook 24, pp. 93ff., Campbell Collection; and interview with Gray Eagle, box 104, notebook 54, Campbell Collection.

27. Telegram, Miles to Terry, Cantonment on Tongue River, Dec. 20, 1876, RG 393, Records of U.S. Army Continental Commands: Special Files, Hq. Division of the Missouri, M1495, Roll 4, Frame 573, NARA.

28. Telegram, Miles to Terry, Cantonment on Tongue River, Dec. 20, 1876, RG 393, Records of U.S. Army Continental Commands: Special Files, Hq. Division of the Missouri, M1495, Roll 4, Frame 573, NARA.

29. Robert P. Higheagle, box 104, folder 21, Campbell Collection.

30. Lt. R. H. Day to Post Adjutant Fort Buford, Fort Peck, April 14, 1877, RG 393, Division of the Missouri Special Files, M1495, Roll 4, Frame 1016, NARA. An Indian who was present at the council described it to the officer in charge of a detachment at the trading post of Fort Peck.

2. JAMES MORROW WALSH

1. The only reliable biography of Walsh is a slim 25-page unpaginated brochure: Brian Porter, *Major James Morrow Walsh of the North West Mounted Police* (Kingston Historical Society, 2005). Two others employ fictional dialogue and other such devices: Anderson, *Sitting Bull's Boss*, and Allan, *White Sioux*. The *Dictionary of Canadian Biography* 13 (1901–10) contains a substantial biographical entry online.
2. *New York Herald*, October 22, 1877.
3. Walsh Scrapbook in Walsh Papers, Provincial Archives of Manitoba, Winnipeg (hereafter cited as the Walsh Papers). Walsh collected news clippings but did not identify them. This was filed from Wolf Point, Montana, on June 26, year not recorded but probably 1879 or 1880. The newspaper is probably the *Chicago Times*, and the correspondent John F. Finerty.
4. A wealth of journals, reminiscences, memoirs, and histories recount the epic story of the March West. Three in particular, which point to many others, are worth citing: Atkin, *Maintaining the Right*, chap. 4; Dempsey, *Men in Scarlet*; and, long the standard, Turner, *North-West Mounted Police*.
5. *New York Herald*, October 22, 1877.
6. Lt. Col. H. Richardson to Assistant Commissioner A. G. Irvine at Fort Macleod, Department of Justice, Ottawa, May 26, 1876, in Fred. White to Major Irvine, Assistant Commissioner NWMP, Ottawa, August 11, 1877, in Report of the Commissioner, North-West Mounted Police, 1877, in *Opening Up the West*, 42.
7. Turner, *North-West Mounted Police*, 1:300.
8. Commissioner James Macleod to Hon. Alexander Mackenzie, Ottawa, May 30, 1877, in Report of the Commissioner, North-West Mounted Police, 1877, in *Opening Up the West*, 34–35.
9. Dispatch from Fort Walsh, May 8, 1877, in *Fort Benton Record*, May 11, 1877.
10. Reconstructing the meeting with Sitting Bull is difficult because Walsh's official report has not survived. A detailed account is in

Turner, *North-West Mounted Police*, 1: 318–22, but no sources are cited. The most comprehensive is in Walsh to My Dear Cora, May 21, 1890, Walsh Papers. This is a long letter in which Walsh sought to tell his daughter about his service in the police. It is highly boastful, often exaggerated, sometimes untruthful. Even so, it contains much information that can be checked against other sources. It will hereafter be cited as the Cora Letter. A short account by one of the constables appears in "Trooper," Fort Walsh, May 30, 1877, in *Fort Benton Record*, June 15, 1877. See also Shepherd, "When Sitting Bull Came to Canada." I portray Walsh and his men as attired in scarlet coats and white helmets. This uniform is not suitable for the outdoor life the police led and likely yielded to more substantial attire. But they wore it in the "March West," Turner labels them redcoats, and the police had learned that the uniform impressed the Indians as symbolic of the White Mother. Moreover, at a crucial council conducted with the Sitting Bull Lakotas on June 2, 1877, less than a month later, police surgeon Richard Nevitt sketched the gathering and clearly showed the police in this uniform, including helmets and the celebrated "pillbox" hats. Nevitt was not present but made his sketch based on guidance from participants. Although the respected police expert George Kush thinks the police probably wore blue patrol jackets, I have concluded that, when Indians were to be encountered, the police donned the uniform most likely to gain respect.

11. These events are drawn from Walsh's account in the Cora Letter and from Turner, *North-West Mounted Police*, 1:319–23. Turner's account closely parallels Walsh's and probably relied heavily on the Cora Letter. "Trooper," Fort Walsh, May 30, 1877, in *Fort Benton Record*, June 15, 1877, and *Bismarck Tribune*, July 11, 1877. Jerome Stillson in *New York Herald*, October 22, 1877.

12. Marty, "Abbott Martin Visits Sitting Bull." *Bismarck Tribune*, June 1 and 18, 1877. *Helena Herald*, July 5, 1877.

13. Irvine to Secretary of State R. W. Scott in Ottawa, Fort Walsh, June 6, 1877, in *Opening Up the West*, 35–37.

14. Detailed minutes of the meeting were kept by Irvine's adjutant, Capt. E. Dalrymple Clark, and printed in *Opening Up the West*, 37–41. An extended account of the journey and council, including direct quotations from Irvine, are in Turner, *North-West Mounted Police*, 1:326–

32. This account contains material not in the official account but also material contradicted by the official account.

15. F. R. Plunkett, British Chargé d'Affaires, to Secretary of State, Washington, June 20, 1877, RG 94, OAG LR (Main Series), 1871–80, File 4163 AGO 1876 (Sioux War Papers), M666, Roll 282, Frame 119, NARA.

16. Sherman to Secretary of War G. W. McCrary, Cantonment on Tongue River, Mont., July 16, 1877, RG 94, OAG LR (Main Series), 1871–80, File 4163 AGO 1876 (Sioux War Papers), M666, Roll 282, Frame 184.

17. The details of the formation of the commission are well–covered in Wilson, "Refugee Crisis."

18. Jerome Stillson describes the journey in great detail. New York Herald, October 22, 1877.

3. THE SITTING BULL COMMISSION

1. U.S. Consul James W. Taylor to Assistant Secretary of State F. W. Seward, Winnipeg, July 24, 1877, RG 94 OAG LR (Main Series) 1871–80, File 4163 AGO 1876 (Sioux War Papers), M666, Roll 282, Frame 212, NARA.

2. Untitled, undated manuscript in the Walsh Papers. Walsh calls this tribal law and describes offenses and penalties.

3. Walsh's report does not appear in the official records, but the correspondent of the New York Herald traveling with the commission, Jerome Stillson, obtained a copy and reproduced it in his account of the meeting. Walsh to Macleod, Fort Walsh, October 12, 1877, New York Herald, October 22, 1877.

4. Walsh deals with this issue in the Cora Letter.

5. Greene, Nez Perce Summer.

6. New York Herald, October 22, 1877. In his Cora Letter, Walsh weaves a fanciful tale of his efforts to restrain the Lakotas from dashing to the aid of the Nez Perces. He does not mention this in his official report.

7. Macleod to Minister of the Interior David Mills at Ottawa, Fort Macleod, October 27, 1877, in Report of the Commissioner, North-West Mounted Police, 1877, in Opening Up the West, 45–47.

8. Both journalists accompanying the commission, Jerome Stillson of the New York Herald and Charles Diehl of the Chicago Times, included this item in their first comprehensive dispatches from Fort Walsh. New York Herald, October 22, 1877. Chicago Times, October 22, 1877.

9. Walsh to Macleod, Fort Walsh, October 16, 1877, in New York Herald, October 22, 1877.

10. This account of the meeting is drawn from the following sources: Official Report of the Terry Commission in Secretary of the Interior, *Annual Report* (1877), 719–28; Report of the Commissioner, North-West Mounted Police, 1877, in *Opening Up the West*, 42–52; Jerome Stillson in *New York Herald*, October 22 and 23, 1877; and Charles Diehl in *Chicago Times*, October 22, 1877. An especially good account of the diplomacy as played out in Washington DC is Pennanen, "Sitting Bull."

11. Nevitt to My dear Lizzie, Fort Walsh, October 18, 1877, Nevitt Papers, box 2, folder 9. Glenbow Museum, Calgary.

12. *Chicago Times*, November 19, 1877.

13. *New York World*, November 9, 1877.

14. *New York World*, November 12, 1877.

15. Macleod to Hon. Alexander Mackenzie, Ottawa, May 30, 1877, in *Opening Up the West*, 34.

16. Campbell interview with Old Bull, box 105, notebook 11, Campbell Collection. Turner, *North-West Mounted Police*, 1:400.

17. Dispatch from Fort Walsh, November 29, 1877, in *Bismarck Tribune*, December 20, 1877. Other sources for the northward movement: *Bismarck Tribune*, January 24, 1878; *New York World*, December 6, 1877; Col. N. A. Miles to AAG DD, Hq. Dist. of the Yellowstone, Fort Keogh, c. January 6, 1878, RG 94, OAG LR (main series), 1872–80, file 4163, AGO 1876 (Sioux War Papers) M666, Roll 284, frame 103, NARA; Lt. Col. Daniel Huston, Sixth Infantry, to AAG DD, Fort Buford, January 17, 1878, Roll 284, frame 148. *New York Herald*, c. August 10, 1878, citing dispatch from Helena, August 9, Walsh Scrapbook, Walsh Papers.

18. Miles to AAG DD, Hq. Dist. of the Yellowstone, Fort Keogh, c. January 6, 1878, RG 94, OAG LR (Main Series), 1871–80, file 4163, AGO 1876 (Sioux War Papers) M666, Roll 284, frame 67, NARA.

19. *Bismarck Tribune*, January 24, 1878. Miles to AAG DD, Hq. Dist. of the Yellowstone, Fort Keogh, January 12, 1878, RG 94, OAG LR (Main Series), 1871–80, file 4163 AGO 1876 (Sioux Wars Papers) M666, Roll 284, frame 141; telegram, Miles to AAG DD, Fort Keogh, January 13, 1878, Roll 284, frame 67; Dispatch from Fort Keogh, January 13, 1878, Roll 284, frame 67; Dispatch from Fort Keogh, January 15, 1878, Roll 284, frame 67, NARA.

20. Sherman to Sheridan, February 9, 1878, RG 94, LR (Main Series), 1871–80, file 4163, AGO 1876 (Sioux Wars Papers), M666, roll 284, frame 190, NARA.

21. Miles to Macleod at Fort Walsh, Hq. Dist. of the Yellowstone, Fort Keogh, June 26, 1879, RG 393, Records of U.S. Army Continental Com-

mands: Special Files, Hq. Military Division of the Missouri, M1495, Roll 5, Frame 440, NARA. Supt. J. M. Walsh to CO NWMP at Fort Walsh, Wood Mountain, July 22, 1879, forwarded by Commissioner James F. Macleod, RG 10, Records of the Indian Affairs Branch, vol. 3652, file 8589, pt. 1, NAC (C-10114).

22. Draft report, "Lakota Indians," Department of the Interior, April 24, 1878, Walsh Papers.

23. *Chicago Times*, May 21, 1878.

24. W. S. Campbell interview with Old Bull, box 105, notebook 11, Campbell Collection; interview with Bob Tail Bull, box 105, notebook 16, Campbell Collection.

4. FALL AND RISE

1. Walsh to CO Fort Walsh, Wood Mountain Post, October 8, 1878, Walsh Papers.

2. Walsh Papers.

3. Draft report, Walsh [to CO Fort Walsh], Wood Mountain, November 2, 1878, Walsh Papers.

4. Draft report, Walsh [to CO Fort Walsh], Wood Mountain, November 9, 1878, Walsh Papers.

5. Draft report, Walsh [to CO Fort Walsh], Wood, Mountain, December 10, 1878, Walsh Papers.

6. Walsh to CO Fort Walsh, Wood Mountain Post, January 25, 1879, *Papers Relating to the Lakota Indians Who Have Taken Refuge in Canadian Territory*, RG 7, Records of the Governor General's Office, G21, file 2001, pt. 3d, NAC.

7. Walsh to Assistant Commissioner NWMP at Fort Walsh, Wood Mountain Post, March 24, 1879, RG 7, G21, vol. 318, file 2001, pt. 3b, NAC.

8. Walsh to Assistant Commissioner NWMP at Fort Walsh, Wood Mountain Post, March 24, 1879, RG 7, G21, vol. 318, file 2001, pt. 3b, NAC.

9. *Chicago Tribune*, July 5, 1879. Saum, "Stanley Huntley Interviews Sitting Bull: Event, Pseudo-Event, or Fabrication?" It was an event.

10. Sherman to Sheridan, July 19, 1879, Sherman-Sheridan Letters, vol. 2, Sheridan Papers, Library of Congress.

11. Agent W. Bird to Commissioner of Indian Affairs, Fort Peck Agency, Montana, Poplar River, April 19, 1879, in SW, AR (1879), 59–60.

12. Terry to AG, MDM Chicago, Hq. DD St. Paul, May 30, 1879; Telegram, Terry to Miles at Fort Keogh, St. Paul, June 5, 1879, SW, AR (1879), 60, 61.

13. *Manitoba Free Press* (Winnipeg), August 8, 1879.

14. MS, untitled, undated, in Walsh Papers.

15. This episode is referred to in a number of sources, but is detailed by one Norman Marion, newly arrived in Winnipeg from Wood Mountain: *Manitoba Free Press* (Winnipeg), September 29, 1879.

16. *Chicago Times*, July 23, 1879.

17. Telegram, Miles to AAG DD, Camp opposite Frenchman's Creek, July 18, 1879, RG 393, Records of U.S. Army Continental Commands, Special Files, Hq. Military Division of the Missouri, M1495, Roll 51, Frame 205, NARA. John F. Finerty, in *Chicago Times*, July 23, 1879. Tate, "Scouting." An unusually detailed account of the fight was given to Major Walsh by Chief Big Road. Walsh to CO NWMP, Wood Mountain Post, July 22, 1879, RG 10, Records of the Indian Affairs Branch, vol. 3652, file 8589, NAC (C-10114).

18. See for example Report of a Committee of the Privy Council of Canada, approved by the Governor General on August 25, 1879, transmitted to the U.S. Secretary of State by Sir Edward Thornton on September 8, 1879, RG 94, OAG LR (Main Series), 1871–80, AGO 1876 (Sioux War Papers) M666, Roll 287, Frame 7. Report of a Committee of the Privy Council of Canada, approved by the Governor General, September 22, 1879, transmitted to the U.S. Secretary of State by Sir Edward Thornton, September 30, 1879, RG 94, OAG LR (Main Series), 1871–80, AGO 1876 (Sioux War Papers) M666, Roll 287, Frame 287, NARA.

19. Supt. J. M. Walsh to CO NWMP, Fort Walsh, July 25, 1879, forwarded by Commissioner James F. Macleod, RG 10, Records of the Indian Affairs Branch, vol. 3652, file 8589, pt. 1, NAC (C10114). *Chicago Times*, August 19, 1879.

20. Finerty, Wood Mountain, July 30, in *Chicago Times*, August 19, 1879.

21. Walsh to CO NWMP, Fort Walsh, July 25, 1879, RG 10, Records of the Indian Affairs Branch, vol. 3652, file 8589, pt. 1. NAC (C10114).

22. Miles to AAG DD, Camp on Rocky Creek, July 28, 1879, RG 393, Records of U.S. Army Continental Commands: Special Files, Hq. Military Division of the Missouri, M1495, Roll 5, Frame 380, NARA. *Chicago Times*, August 9, 1879 (dispatch from Miles's camp at Rocky Creek by Finerty, July 29).

23. Telegram, Walsh to Miles, Wood Mountain Post, July 31, 1879, via Fort Buford August 8, RG 393, Records of U.S. Army Continental Com-

mands: Special Files, Hq. Military Division of the Missouri, M1495, Roll 5, Frame 408, NARA.

5. CREEPING UNCERTAINTY

1. MS, untitled, undated, in Walsh Papers. Lt. Edward Chynoweth to Post Adjutant Fort Yates, April 15, 1880, RG 94, OAG LR (Main Series), 1871–80, file 4163 AGO 1876 (Sioux War Papers), M666, roll 288, frame 22, NARA. Annual Report of Supt. J. M. Walsh, December 31, 1880, in *Opening Up the West*, 25–29.

2. MS, untitled, undated, in Walsh Papers. Lt. Edward Chynoweth to Post Adjutant Fort Yates, April 15, 1880, RG 94, OAG LR (Main Series), 1871–80, file 4163 AGO 1876 (Sioux War Papers), M666, roll 288, frame 22, NARA. Annual Report of Supt. J. M. Walsh, December 31, 1880, in *Opening Up the West*, 25–29.

3. Minutes of a Talk at Fort Buford, May 23, 1880, with Young Eagle [sic], young Hunkpapa warrior and adopted son of Sitting Bull, sent by Sitting Bull to ascertain terms of surrender, RG 94, OAG, LR (Main Series), 1871–80, file 4163 AGO 1876 (Sioux War Papers), M666, roll 288, frame 104, NARA.

4. Walsh to Macleod, Wood Mountain Post, June 5, 1880, RG 10, Records of the Indian Affairs Branch, vol. 3652, file 8589, pt. 1, NAC (C-10114). Annual Report of Supt. J. M. Walsh, Brockville, Ontario, December 31, 1880, in *Opening Up the West*, 37. The correspondent of the *Manitoba Free Press* witnessed this entire affair and published the details in his paper, which were picked up by the *Chicago Tribune* on June 4, 1880.

5. I have found no direct evidence of the purpose of Walsh's removal. But the record for the rest of 1880 contains enough disparaging comments by high officials that Walsh bore the responsibility for Sitting Bull's intransigence to support my belief. Some of this will be cited as the narrative continues.

6. Annual Report of Supt. J. M. Walsh, Brockville, Ontario, December 31, 1880, in *Opening Up the West*, 28. Walsh to Minister of the Interior, Wood Mountain Post, July 3, 1880; Walsh to CO Fort Walsh, Wood Mountain Post, July 14, 1880, both in RG 10, Records of the Indian Affairs Branch, vol. 3691, file 13,893, "Northwest Territories," NAC (C-10121).

7. Walsh to Minister of the Interior, Brockville, Ontario, September 9, 1880, RG 10, Records of the Indian Affairs Branch, vol. 3691, file 13,893, "Northwest Territories," NAC (C-10121).

8. Irvine to Minister of the Interior, Fort Walsh, December 8, 1880, RG 18, Records of the Royal Canadian Mounted Police, B3, vol. 2185, Fort Walsh Letter Book, November 1880–March 1881, NAC (T-6268). This is one of the few instances of a document from the police files that escaped the fire that destroyed most of them.

9. Aide de Camp Smith by command of Terry to Brotherton, Hq. DD St. Paul, October 15, 1880, RG 94, OAG LR (Main Series), 1871–80, File 4163 AGO 1876 (Sioux War Papers), M666, Roll 288. NARA. Allison published his story in *South Dakota Historical Collections* and later as *The Surrender of Sitting Bull: Being a Full and Complete History of the Negotiations Conducted by Scout Allison Which Resulted in the Surrender of Sitting Bull and his Entire Band of Hostile Sioux in 1881.*This short book contains much information of value, but it is frequently contradicted by Allison's own detailed reports to Brotherton. I have occasionally drawn from the book but relied more heavily on the official record. The book portrays Allison's actions in dramatic prose, greatly exaggerated and at times fabricated.

10. Allison to CO Fort Buford, Fort Buford, October 12, 1880, RG 94, OAG LR (Main Series), 1871–80, File 4163 AGO 1876 (Sioux War Papers), M666, Roll 288, Frame 400. Terry to AAG MDM, October 13, 1880, RG 94, OAG LR (Main Series), 1871–80, File 4163 AGO 1876 (Sioux War Papers), M666, Roll 288, frame 350, NARA. Allison's report to Terry differs fundamentally from the account he left in his book.

11. Telegram, Brotherton to AAAG DD, Fort Buford, November 7, 1880, RG 94, OAG LR (Main Series), 1871–80, File 4163 AGO 1876 (Sioux War Papers), M666, Roll 288, frame 472, NARA. In his book Allison makes no mention of this council.

12. Telegram, Terry to AAG MDM., St. Paul, October 31, 1880, RG 94, OAG LR (Main Series), 1871–80, File 4163 AGO 1876 (Sioux War Papers), M666, Roll 288, frame 453, NARA. Crozier to CO Fort Macleod, Wood Mountain, October 14, 1880, RG 10, Records of the Indian Affairs Branch, vol. 3652, file 8589, pt.1, NAC (C-101114).

13. Telegram, Brotherton to AAG DD St. Paul, Fort Buford, November 7, 1880, RG 94, OAG LR (Main Series), 1871–80, File 4163 AGO 1876 (Sioux War Papers), M666, Roll 288, Frame 472, NARA.

14. Telegram, Brotherton to AAG DD St. Paul, Fort Buford, November 7, 1880, RG 94, OAG LR (Main Series), 1871–80, File 4163 AGO 1876 (Sioux War Papers), M666, Roll 288, Frame 472, NARA; November 27, 1880, Frame 583, NARA; and December 4. 1880, Frame 49, NARA.

15. Telegram, Brotherton to AAG DD St. Paul, Fort Buford, November 7, 1880, RG 94, OAG LR (Main Series), 1871–80, File 4163 AGO 1876 (Sioux War Papers), M666, Roll 288, Frame 472, NARA; December 17, 1880, Frame 119, NARA.

16. Telegram, Ilges to AAG DD, Cantonment Poplar River, December 25, 1880, RG 94, OAG LR (Main Series), 1871–80, File 4163 AGO 1876 (Sioux War Papers), M666, Roll 289, NARA.

17. Telegram, Terry to Sheridan, January 3, 1881, forwarding telegram, Ilges to Terry, Camp Poplar River, January 2, 1881, *Chicago Times*, January 4, 1881. NARA.

18. Telegram, Terry to AAG MDM, St. Paul, January 11, 1881; Telegram, Brek AAG DD to Ilges at Camp Poplar River, January 10, 1881; Telegram, Ilges to AAG DD, Camp Poplar River, January 22, 1880; all in RG 393, Records of U.S. Army Continental Commands, Special Files, Hq. MDM, M1495, Roll 5, NARA. *Chicago Times*, January 20, 1881.

19. Telegram, Brotherton to Terry, Fort Buford, February 6, 1881, RG 393, U.S. Army Continental Commands: Special Files, Hq. Military Division of the Missouri, M1495, Roll 5, Frame 622. Telegram, same to same, February 8, 1881, RG 393, U.S. Army Continental Commands: Special Files, Hq. Military Division of the Missouri, M1495, Roll 5, Frame 613. Telegram, same to same, Fort Buford, February 21, 1881, RG 393, U.S. Army Continental Commands: Special Files, Hq. Military Division of the Missouri, M1495, Roll 5, Frame 664, NARA.

20. Irvine to Frederick White in Ottawa, Fort Walsh, February 2, 1881. RG 10, Records of the Indian Affairs Branch, vol. 3652, File 8589, pt. 1, NAC (C-10114).

21. Crozier to Irvine, Wood Mountain, February 8, 1881, RG 10, Records of the Indian Affairs Branch, vol. 3652, File 8589, pt. 1, NAC (C-10114).

6. INDECISION

1. Annual Report of Superintendent L.N.F. Crozier, Wood Mountain, December 1880. North-West Mounted Police Annual Reports for 1880, in *Opening Up the West*, 32.

2. Brotherton to Terry, Fort Buford, February 8, 1881; same to same, February 21, 1881, RG 393, Records of U.S. Army Continental Commands: Special Files, Hq. MDM (M1495, Roll 5, Frames 613 and 664), NARA. Telegram, Capt. O. B. Read to AAG DD, Poplar River, March 29 1881, RG 393, Records of U.S. Army Continental Commands: Special Files,

Hq. Military Division of the Missouri, M1495, Roll 5, Frame 695, NARA. Irving to Minister of the Interior, Fort Walsh, March 22, 1881, confidential, RG 18, Records of the RCMP, B3, Vol. 2185, Fort Walsh Letter Book, November 1880–March 1881, NAC (T-6269).

3. Crozier to Irvine, Wood Mountain, April 3, 1881, RG 10, Records of the Indian Affairs Branch, vol. 3691, file 13,893, "Northwest Territories," NAC (C-10121). Crozier to CO Poplar River, Wood Mountain, March 25, 1881, RG 393, Records of U.S. Army Continental Commands, LR Camp Poplar River, September 1880–83, box 1, NARA. Telegram, Reid to AAG DD, Poplar River, March 29, 1881, RG 393, Records of U.S. Army Continental Commands: Special Files, Hq. MDM, M1495, Roll 5, frame 695, NARA.

4. Crozier to Brotherton, Wood Mountain, April 5, 1881, RG 10, Records of the Indian Affairs Branch, vol. 3652, file 8580, pt. 1, NAC (C-101114).

5. Crozier to CO Poplar River, Wood Mountain, April 5, 1881; Captain O. B. Read to CO Fort Buford, Camp Poplar River, April 9, 1881; Telegram, Brotherton to Terry, Fort Buford, April 11, 1881; same to same, April 12, 1881. RG 393, Records of U.S. Army Continental Commands: Special Files, Hq. MDM, M1495, Roll 5, NARA. Brotherton to Crozier, April 11, 1881, RG 10, Records of the Indian Affairs Branch, vol. 3652, file 8589, pt. 1, NAC (C-10114).

6. Crozier to Irvine, Wood Mountain, April 19, 1881, RG 10, Records of the Indian Affairs Branch, vol. 3652, file 8589, pt. 1, NAC (C-10114). For Macdonell, see Deposition of Captain Alexander A. Macdonell, Regina, Sask., August 25, 1888, in *Legaré v. United States*, RG 123, Records of the U.S. Court of Claims, General Jurisdiction, No. 15713, NARA. It is uncharacteristic of One Bull to have lied to his uncle. He would have told the truth, and it would have been that at Fort Buford the Lakota prisoners were being well treated.

7. Crozier to Irvine, Wood Mountain, April 19, 1881, RG 10, Records of the Indian Affairs Branch, vol. 3652, file 8589, pt. 1, NAC (C-10114).

8. Crozier to Captain O. B. Read at Poplar, Wood Mountain, April 21, 1881, RG 393, Records of U.S. Army Commands, LR Camp Poplar River September 1880–June 1883, box 1, NARA. Crozier to Brotherton, Wood Mountain, April 21, 1881, RG 393, Records of U.S. Army Continental Commands, Hq. Military Division of the Missouri, M495, Roll 5, Frame 722, NARA. Telegram. Terry to AAG MDM, St. Paul, April 25, 1881, May 26, 1881, RG 393, Records of U.S. Army Continental Commands, Hq. Military Division of the Missouri, M495, Roll 5, Frames 719, 770, NARA.

Telegram, Brotherton to Terry, Fort Buford, May 4, 1881, RG 393, Records of U.S. Army Continental Commands, Hq. Military Division of the Missouri, M495, Roll 5, Frame 751, NARA.

9. Crozier to Irvine, Wood Mountain Post, April 19, 1881, RG 10, Records of the Indian Affairs Branch, vol. 3652, File 8589, pt. 1, NAC (C10114). *Dictionary of Canadian Biography* 13 (1901–10), Crozier online.

10. Crozier to Irvine, Wood Mountain, April 3, 1881, RG 10, Records of the Indian Affairs Branch, vol. 3691, file 13,893, "Northwest Territories," NAC (C-10121). Crozier to CO Poplar River, Wood Mountain, March 25, 1881, RG 393, Records of U.S. Army Continental Commands, LR Camp Poplar River, September 1880–83, box 1, NARA. Telegram, Reid to AAG DD, Poplar River, March 29, 1881, RG 393, Records of U.S. Army Continental Commands: Special Files, Hq. MDM, M1495, Roll 5, frame 695, NARA.

11. Crozier to Read, Wood Mountain, April 21, 1881, RG 393, LR Camp Poplar River, box 1, NARA. Crozier to Brotherton, same date. RG 94, AGO LR 1871–80, file 4163, AGO 1876, M666, roll 290, frame 19, NARA.

12. Crozier to Irvine, Wood Mountain, May 1, 1881, RG 10, Records of the Indian Affairs Branch, vol. 3691, file 13,893, "Northwest Territories," NAC (C-10121).

13. MS, untitled, undated, in Walsh Papers.

14. *Toronto Citizen*, undated clipping in Walsh Papers.

15. MS, William Morris Graham, "Memoirs," Graham Papers, box 1, folder 2B, pp. 267–71; "Father Hugounard Gives Interesting Address," undated newspaper clipping, c. 1916, probably Regina newspaper. Graham Papers, M8097. Both in Glenbow Museum, Calgary.

16. Dewdney to Superintendent General of Indian Affairs Ottawa, Shoal Lake, June 7, 1881, RG 10, Records of the Indian Affairs Branch, vol. 3652, file 8589, pt. 1, NAC (C-10114). This is a very long document, and most of what follows is drawn from this source.

17. Robert P. Higheagle, MS, 84, Campbell Collection, box 104, folder 21. In later years, it was commonly said that Crow Foot grew up too fast. At age fifteen he was in his father's cabin when the police came to arrest him and died in the gunfire that followed.

18. Edgar Dewdney, Commissioner of Indian Affairs, Northwest Territories, to Superintendent General of Indian Affairs Ottawa, Shoal Lake, June 7, 1881, RG 10, Records of the Indian Affairs Branch, vol. 3652, file 8589, pt. 1, NAC (C-10114). All the above detail is contained in this single report.

19. Undated clipping from *Toronto Globe* in Walsh scrapbook, Walsh Papers.

20. Undated clipping from *Toronto Globe* in Walsh scrapbook, Walsh Papers.

7. JEAN LOUIS

1. Black, *History of Saskatchewan*, 189.

2. Most of this chapter is based on the lengthy trial transcript of Legaré's effort to obtain reimbursement for the expenses incurred in persuading and transporting the Sitting Bull Indians to Fort Buford. *Legaré v. United States*. RG 123, Records of the U.S. Court of Claims, General Jurisdiction, No. 15713 , NARA. Another lengthy source is Legaré to W. M. Camp, Willow Bunch, Sask., October 27, 1910, W. M. Camp Papers, box 1, folder 14, Brigham Young University. Camp was a collector of papers on the American West. This letter is difficult to use because of Legaré's near illiteracy.

3. Legaré deposition, Regina, Sask, August 17, 1888, in *Legaré v. United States*.

4. W. S. Campbell interview with Old Bull, Campbell Collection, box 105, notebook 12.

5. Jean Louis Legaré deposition, Regina, Sask, August 17, 1888, in *Legaré v. United States*.

6. Telegram, Brotherton to Terry, Fort Buford, May 6, 1881, RG 94, AGO LR 1871–80, File 4163, M666, Roll 290, Frame 123, NARA. *Bismarck Tribune*, July 3 and August 5, 1881. *Chicago Times*, June 11, 1881.

7. Telegram, Brotherton to AAG DD, Fort Buford, May 26, 1881, RG 393, Records of U.S. Army Continental Commands: Special Files, Hq. MDM, M1495, Roll 5, Frame 770, NARA.

8. *Chicago Times*, June 11, 1881.

9. Legaré to Brotherton, July 12, 1881, in *St. Paul Pioneer Press*, July 18, 1881. Telegram, Brotherton to Terry, Fort Buford, July 14, 1881, RG 393, Records of U.S. Army Continental Commands: Special Files, Hq. MDM, M1495, Roll 5, Frame 819, NARA.

10. Brotherton to Legare, Fort Buford, July 15,1881, in *Legare v. United States*.

11. Clifford's experiences and observations while in Sitting Bull's camp are detailed in an article he wrote for the Buffalo *Sunday News*, reprinted

in the *Army and Navy Journal* 19 (August 13, 1881): 24. *St. Paul Pioneer Press*, July 20, 1881.

12. Telegram, Whipple AAG to AGUSA, Hq. MDM Chicago, July 26, 1881, forwarding telegrams from Terry and Brotherton, RG 94, OAG (Main Series), 1871–80, File 4163 AGO 1876 (Sioux War Papers), M666, Roll 290, Frame 383, NARA.

13. *St. Paul Pioneer Press*, July 21 1881. See also for the detailed story Hedren, "Sitting Bull's Surrender."

14. Sources for the week at Fort Buford and the journey down to Bismarck and Fort Yates are *Bismarck Tribune*, August 5, 1881, and *St. Paul Pioneer Press*, August 3, 4, 7, and 14, 1881. Also, *Army and Navy Journal*, August 5, 1881.

15. Creelman, *On The Great Highway*, 301.

EPILOGUE

1. All are in the National Anthropological Archives of the Smithsonian Institution in Washington DC.

2. McLaughlin wrote a well-regarded book about his life at Standing Rock and elsewhere. McLaughlin, *My Friend the Indian*.

3. Senate Reports, 48th Congress, 1st session, no. 283, serial 2164, 80–81.

4. "One Bull's Memoirs," One Bull File. Box 104, folder 11, Campbell Collection.

5. Stillman, *Blood Brothers*.

6. I have recounted this story in *The Last Days*.

7. This account of Sitting Bull's death is drawn from interviews with various participants and observers in the Campbell Collection. In more detail in appears in my book, *Lance and the Shield*, chap. 24.

8. Legaré's story is contained in his suit against the U.S. government. *Legare v. United States*, RG 123, Records of the U.S. Court of Claims, General Jurisdiction, No. 15713, NARA. Also, Legare to W. M. Camp, Willow Bunch, Sask., October 27, 1910, W. M. Camp Papers, box 1, folder 14, Brigham Young University. *Dictionary of Canadian Biography* 14 (1911–20). Online.

9. Walsh's life after his resignation from the police is detailed in *Dictionary of Canadian Biography* 13 (1901–10). Online.

Bibliography

MANUSCRIPTS AND ARCHIVES

University of Oklahoma Library Western History Collection
    Walter S. Campbell Collection

Provincial Archives of Manitoba, Winnipeg
    James M. Walsh Papers

Harold B. Lee Library, Brigham Young University, Provo, Utah
    Walter M. Camp Collection

Glenbow Institute, Calgary, Alberta
    Richard Nevitt Papers
    Edgar Dewdney Papers
    William Morris Graham Papers

U.S. Library of Congress
    Philip H. Sheridan Papers

U.S. National Archives
    RG 75, Records of the Bureau of Indian Affairs, microfilm M234
    RG 393, Records of U.S. Army Continental Commands, Special Files of the Military Division of the Missouri, 1863–85, microfilm M1495
    RG 123, Records of the U.S. Court of Claims, General Jurisdiction.
    RG 94, Letters Received by the Office of the Adjutant General, Microfilm M666.

National Archives of Canada
    RG 7, Records of the Governor General's Office
    RG 10, Records of the Indian Affairs Branch
    RG 18, Records of the Royal Canadian Mounted Police

PUBLISHED WORKS

Allan, Iris. *White Sioux: The Story of Major Walsh of the Mounted Police.* Sidney BC: Gray's, 1969.

Allison, E. H. "The Surrender of Sitting Bull." *South Dakota Historical Collections* 6 (1910–12): 231–70.

Allison, E. H. *The Surrender of Sitting Bull: Being a Full and Complete History of the Negotiations Conducted by Scout Allison Which Resulted in the Surrender of Sitting Bull and his Entire Band of Hostile Sioux in 1881.* Walker Litho. and Printing Co., 1891.

Anderson, Ian. *Sitting Bull's Boss: Above the Medicine Line with James Morrow Walsh.* Surrey BC: Heritage House, 2000.

Atkin, Ronald. *Maintaining the Right: The Early History of the North West Mounted Police, 1873–1900.* New York: John Day, 1973.

Baker, William M. *The Mounted Police and Prairie Society, 1873–1919.* Regina: University of Regina Press, 1998.

Black, Norman H. *History of Saskatchewan and the Old Northwest.* Regina: North West Historical, 1913.

Clow, Richmond L. "Mad Bear: William S. Harney and the Expedition of 1855–1856." *Nebraska History* 61 (Summer 1980): 132–49.

Creelman, James. *On the Great Highway: The Wanderings and Adventures of a Special Correspondent.* Boston: Lothrop, 1901.

Dempsey, Hugh A., ed. *Men in Scarlet.* Calgary: Historical Society of Alberta, 1973.

Denny, Sir Cecil E. *The Law Marches West.* Gloucestershire, UK: Denny, 2000.

Graham W. A. *The Custer Myth: A Source Book of Custeriana.* Harrisburg PA: Stackpole, 1953.

Gray, John S. "Peace-Talkers from Standing Rock Agency." *Westerners Brand Book* 23 (May 1966): 17–29.

———. "Sitting Bull Strikes the Glendive Supply Trains." *Westerners Brand Book* 28 (June 1971): 25–27, 31–32.

Greene, Jerome A. *Nez Perce Summer: The U.S. Army and the Ne Moo Poo Crisis.* Helena: Montana Historical Society Press, 2000.

———. *Yellowstone Command: Colonel Nelson A. Miles and the Great Sioux War.* Lincoln: University of Nebraska Press, 1991.

Hayden, A. L. *The Riders of the Plains: A Record of the Royal Northwest Mounted Police of Canada, 1873–1910.* London: Andrew Melrose, 1911.

Hedren, Paul L. "Sitting Bull's Surrender at Fort Buford: An Episode in American History." *North Dakota History* 62 (Fall 1995): 2–15.

Larpenteur, Charles. *Forty Years a Fur Trader on the Upper Missouri, 1833–1872*. Chicago: Lakeside Classics, R. F. Donnelley & Sons, 1933.

MacBeth, R. G. *Policing the Plains: Being the Real-Life Record of the Famous North-West Mounted Police*. n.p., n.d.

MacEwan, Grant. *Sitting Bull: The Years in Canada*. Edmonton AB: Hurting, 1973.

Macleod, R. C. *The NWMP and Law Enforcement, 1873–1895*. Toronto: University of Toronto Press, 1976.

Manzione, Joseph. *"I Am Looking to the North for My Life": Sitting Bull, 1876–1881*. Salt Lake City: University of Utah Press, 1991.

Marquis, Thomas B. *A Warrior Who Fought Custer*. Minneapolis: Midwest, 1931.

Marty, Martin. "Abbott Martin Visits Sitting Bull." *Annals of the Catholic Indian Missions of America* 2 (January 1878): 7–10.

McLaughlin, James. *My Friend the Indian*. Lincoln: University of Nebraska Press, 1989.

North-West Mounted Police. *Opening Up the West: Being the Official Reports to Parliament of the Activities of the North-West Mounted Police from 1874–1881*. Toronto: Coles, 1973.

Pennanen, Gary. "Sitting Bull: Indian Without a Country." *Canadian Historical Review* 51 (June 1970): 123–40.

Porter, Brian. *Major James Morrow Walsh of the North West Mounted Police*. Kingston Historical Society, 2005.

Robertson, Francis B. "We Are Going to Have a Big Lakota War: Colonel David S. Stanley's Yellowstone Expedition, 1872." *Montana: The Magazine of Western History* 34 (Autumn 1984).

Saum, Lewis O. "Stanley Huntley Interviews Sitting Bull: Event, Pseudo-Event, or Fabrication?" *Montana: The Magazine of Western History* 32 (Spring 1982): 2–15.

Shepherd, George. "When Sitting Bull Came to Canada." *Royal Canadian Mounted Police Quarterly* 9, no. 4 (April 1942): 404–10.

Stillman, Deanne. *Blood Brothers: The Story of the Strange Friendship between Sitting Bull and Buffalo Bill*. New York: Simon and Schuster, 2017.

Tate, Michael. "Scouting with the U.S. Army, 1876–79: The Diary of Fred M. Hans." *South Dakota Historical Quarterly* 40 (1981): 128–34.

Terry, Alfred H. Report of the Commission Appointed by Direction of the President of the United States, Under Instructions of the Honorables the Secretary of War and the Secretary of the Interior to Meet the Sioux Indian Chief Sitting Bull, With a View to Avert Hostile Incursions into the Territory of the United States from the Dominion of Canada, Annual Report of the Secretary of the Interior (1877), 719–28.

Turner, John Peter. *The North-West Mounted Police, 1873–1893*. 2 vols. Ottawa: Kings Printer and Controller of Stationery, 1950.Utley, Robert M. *Cavalier in Buckskin: George Armstrong Custer and the Western Military Frontier*, rev. ed. Norman: University of Oklahoma Press, 2001.

——— . *Frontier Regulars: The United States Army and the Indian, 1866–1891*. New York: Macmillan, 1973.

——— . *The Lance and the Shield: The Life and Times of Sitting Bull*. New York: Henry Holt, 1993.

——— . *The Last Days of the Sioux Nation*. rev. ed. New Haven: Yale University Press, 2004.

Vestal, Stanley. *Sitting Bull: Champion of the Lakotas*. New York: Houghton Mifflin, 1932.

——— . *Warpath: The True Story of the Fighting Sioux, Told in a Biography of Chief White Bull*. Lincoln: University of Nebraska Press, 1984.

Wilkins, Charles. *The Wild Ride: A History of the North-West Mounted Police, 1873–1904*. Vancouver BC: Stanton Atkins & Dosil, 2010.

Wilson, Garrett. "Refugee Crisis." *Canada's History*, February–March 2017 (online at PressReader, February 1, 2017).

Index